AF575518

Vanessa Bell

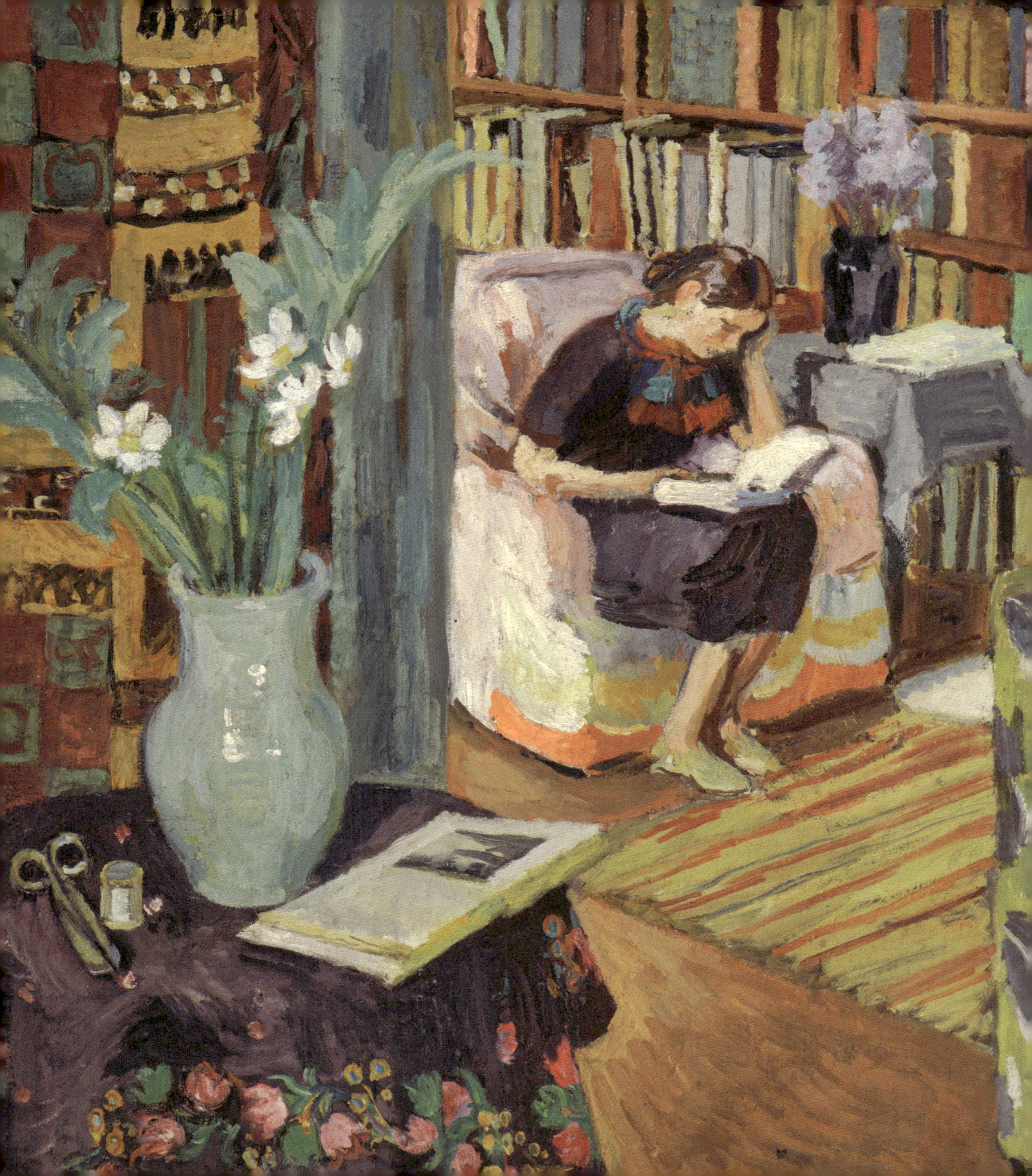

Vanessa Bell

MODERN LIVING

Rosalind McKever

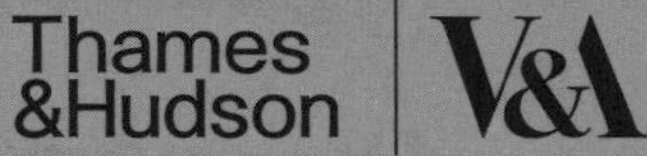

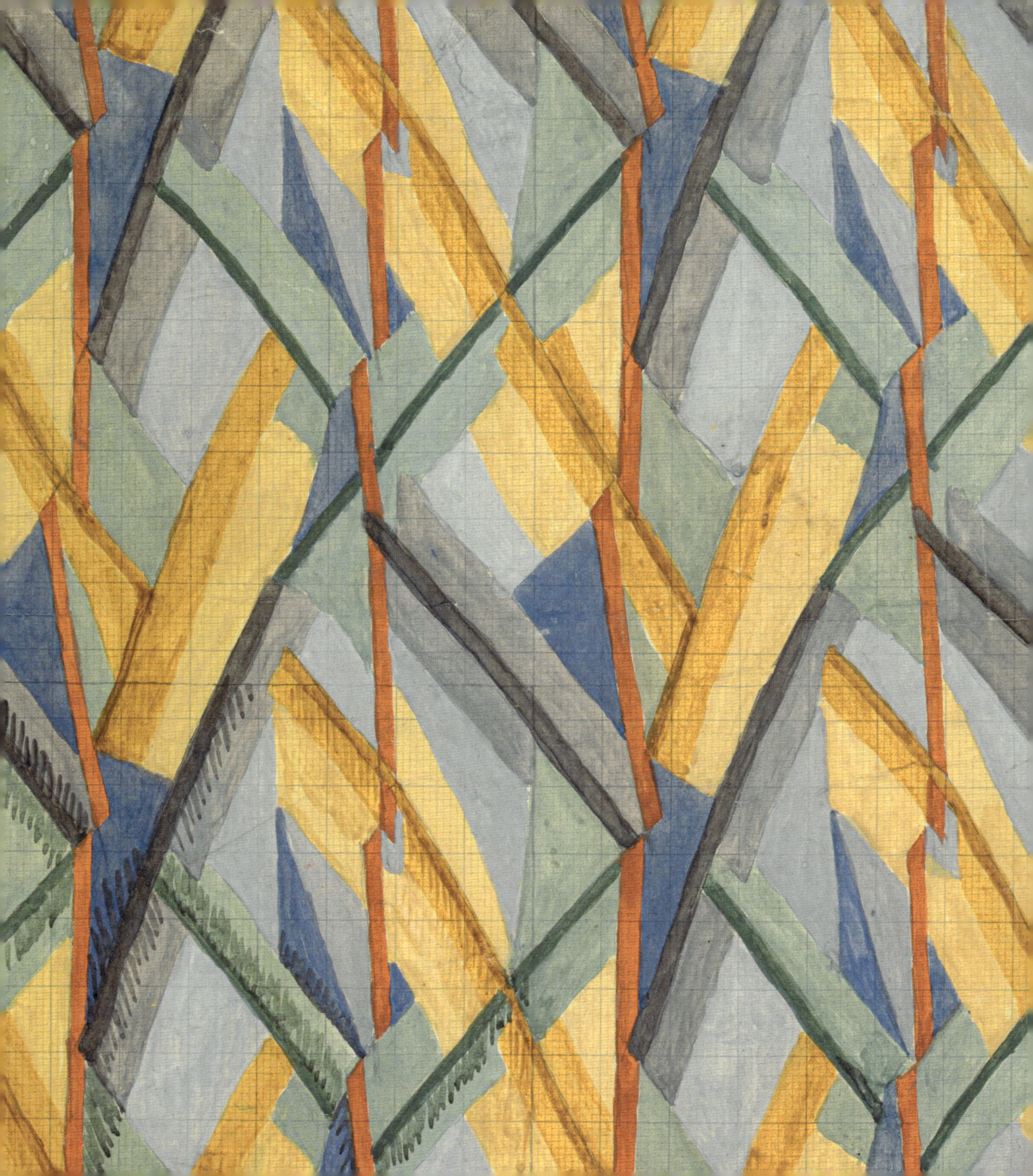

Contents

Introduction

The domestic strain in you is very odd.
How do you account for it? Perhaps it's the sign of real genius.
If you were only very clever you wouldn't care for such things.[1]

Vanessa Bell to Virginia Stephen, 1907

Vanessa Bell (1879–1961) took a radical approach to her life and work as an artist and designer. She subverted social and aesthetic norms, blurred boundaries between modern art and modern living, and championed emotion over narrative in works characterized by abstract form and bold colour. Painting her self-portrait in 1915 (**fig. 1**), Bell positioned herself in front of an arrangement of green and blue, yellow and purple, a background as inscrutable as her expression. Its angular forms do little to suggest the soft furnishings of a domestic space, nor are they clearly identifiable as the stretched canvases that might place her firmly in her studio. And yet, Bell's art has become inextricable from her homelife.

Bell is known to many through the people and places surrounding her. Alongside her sister the author Virginia Woolf (1882–1941), her husband the art critic Clive Bell (1881–1964) and her lovers the artists Roger Fry (1866–1934) and Duncan Grant (1885–1978), she was a central figure in the Bloomsbury group, named after the area of London to which she moved in 1904 and her friends gravitated before and after the First World War. Charleston, her wartime retreat in the Sussex countryside, later became the lifelong home of her blended family. Both her London townhouse and rural farmhouse operated as family living space, studio and canvas. It was not only her own homes that she decorated in keeping with her aesthetic; Bell designed interiors for

Fig. 1 *Self-Portrait*, 1915
Oil on canvas laid on panel,
63.8 × 45.9 cm
Yale Center for British Art
(B1982.16.2)

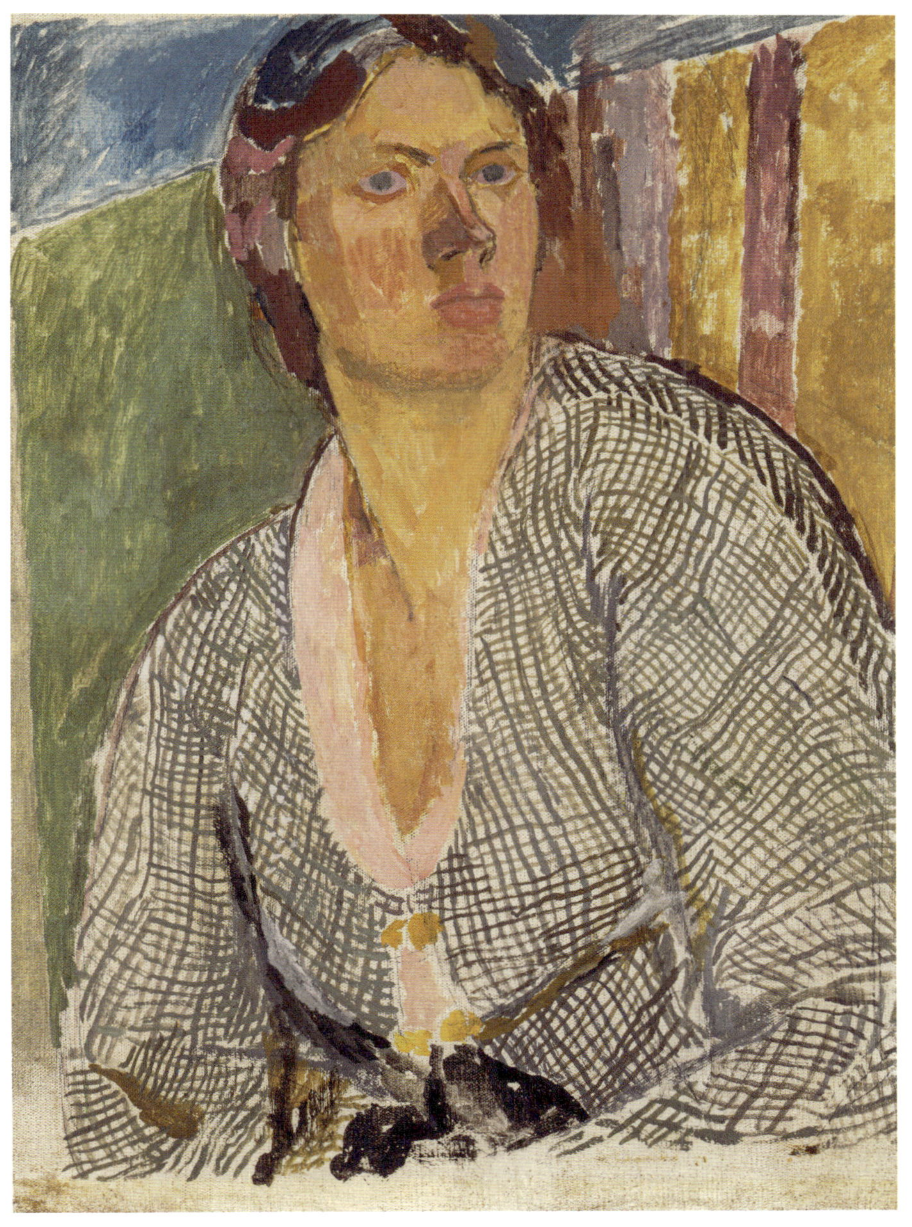

many Bloomsbury group friends, and created homewares, prints and book jackets that would see her designs adorn the walls, dressers and bookshelves of middle-class houses.

Born into an upper-class family, albeit one with artistic and literary connections, Bell countered expectations for women of her status in Victorian Britain. Lacking the same access to educational and artistic institutions as her brothers and male friends, Bell fostered her own communities and created environments where freedom of expression thrived. She was a highly collaborative artist and designer, working closely with other members of the Bloomsbury group, especially Duncan Grant, and many independent makers and major manufacturers. Bell enjoyed success as an artist and designer during her lifetime, and in 1923 the editor of the prestigious *Burlington Magazine* named her 'the most important woman painter in Europe'.[2]

Yet, Bell herself said little about her own work, which was unusual during a period when many modern artists promoted their movements and declared their politics through manifestos. Virginia Woolf memorably characterized her sister's artistic aloofness by writing 'Mrs Bell says nothing.'[3] As the matriarch of Bloomsbury, Bell was self-effacing, promoting Grant's work over her own and prioritizing the needs of her family, especially her sister and children. Bell felt the impact of her familial duties on her art, writing to her daughter in 1941, just before she married, of how 'terribly difficult it is to paint seriously when one is responsible for other things, and hasn't room and space to oneself and we females have to struggle for it all our lives one way or another'.[4]

The greater fame of other Bloomsbury group members, fascination with their personal lives and resulting association of Bell with the decorative and the domestic have threatened to overshadow her artistic career.[5] However, it is precisely her radical domesticity – overturning Victorian models to embrace modern living – which allowed her to establish the home as a crucial site of modernity.

Hyde Park Gate

Born Vanessa Stephen in 1879, her first home was at 22 Hyde Park Gate, a six-storey house close to the Victoria and Albert Museum in affluent southwest London. She would turn 21 at the start of the twentieth century, yet she grew up amid distinctly mid-Victorian decoration of dark walls and woodwork and heavy velvet upholstery, creating an oppressive dreariness exacerbated by poor lighting.[6] Vanessa was the eldest daughter of Leslie and Julia Stephen, sister to Thoby, Virginia and Adrian, and half-sister to George, Stella and Gerald Duckworth, the older children of Julia's previous marriage.

Leslie Stephen (1832–1904) was a writer and the first editor of the *Dictionary of National Biography*, and Julia Prinsep Stephen (1846–1895) was a model for Pre-Raphaelite artists and a niece and goddaughter of pioneering photographer Julia Margaret Cameron (1815–1879), appearing in a number of her photographs (fig. 2). The regular social events they hosted at their home brought their children into contact with late Victorian artistic circles. This family pedigree and social milieu may have emboldened the young Vanessa's aspirations; she could not remember a time when she did not want to be a painter.[7] Although Vanessa and Virginia were taught at home while the brothers went to school, Leslie Stephen recognized his eldest daughter's talents and allowed her to attend one of art teacher Ebenezer Cooke's drawing classes.

When Vanessa was 15, her mother died, and she was given housekeeping responsibilities, which only increased on the death of Stella two years later, in 1897. Mourning closeted Vanessa and Virginia Stephen in the sombre gloom of their home, but George Duckworth insisted Vanessa still be inducted into high society, and escorted her to social events, whether she wished to attend or not.[8]

Escape from domestic responsibility and social tedium came in the form of Arthur Cope's art school in nearby South Kensington:

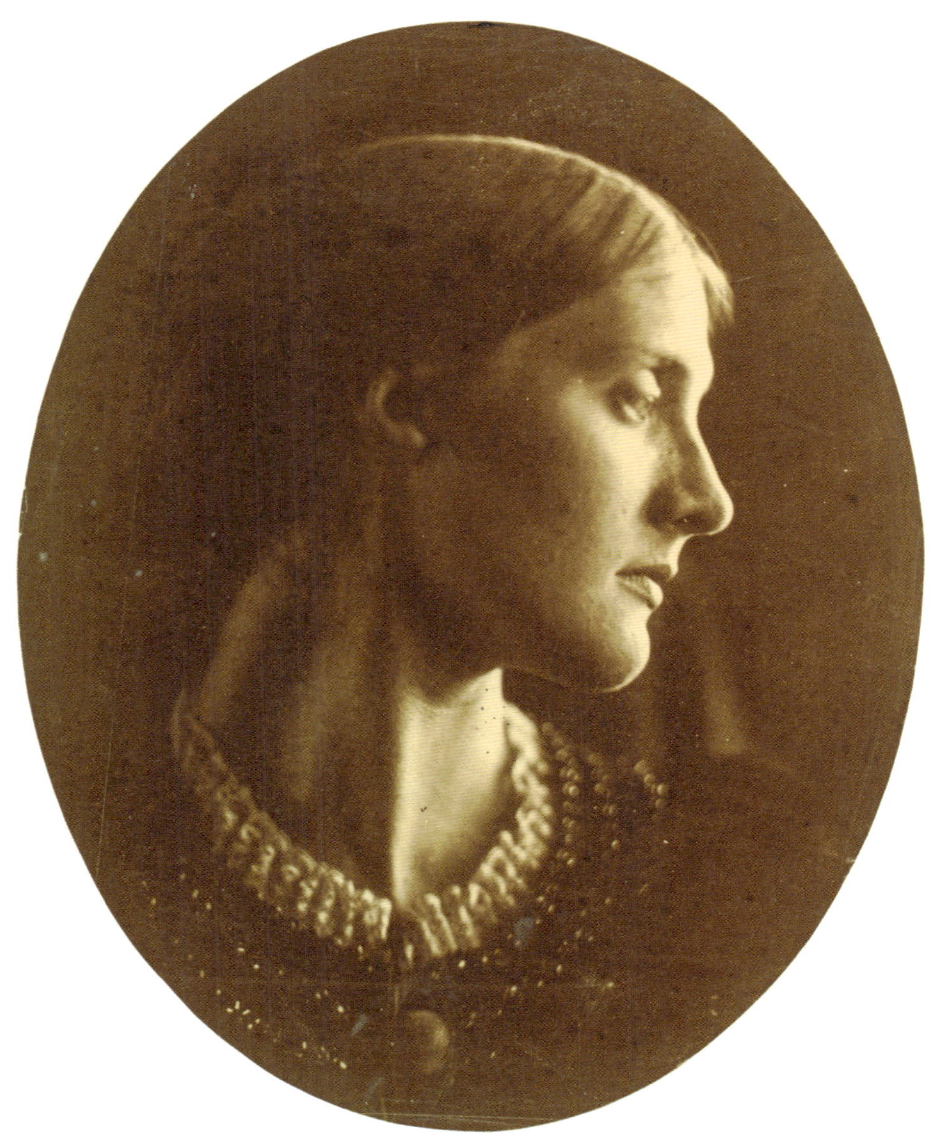

Fig. 2 Julia Margaret Cameron, *Julia Jackson*, 1864
Albumen print, 27.1 × 21.7 cm
Victoria and Albert Museum, London (V&A: 206-1969)
Given by Mrs Margaret Southam, 1941

> When I got into the grubby, shabby, dirty world of art students at South Kensington I wanted nothing else in the way of society. They were separate entirely from my home life and so a great relief. They knew no more about my private life than I about theirs and in their company one could forget oneself and think of nothing but shapes and colours and the absorbing difficulties of oil paint.[9]

In 1901, aged 22, Vanessa Stephen was admitted to the painting school at London's prestigious Royal Academy. The esteemed portraitist John Singer Sargent (1856–1925) was among her tutors, and from him she learned the importance of tone and truthful observation, tenets that would stay with her throughout her career. While the Academy represented artistic convention, Vanessa did not want for avant-garde examples. In these years she was exposed to recent developments in art in London and Paris, including the work of James McNeill Whistler (1834–1903), a central figure in the Aesthetic movement who believed in art for art's sake, and the revolutionary French Impressionists, whom she learned about through the 1903 English translation of Camille Mauclair's influential history.[10] She visited the exhibitions of the New English Art Club, which had been founded in 1886 by artists dissatisfied with the Royal Academy, including the painter (and Whistler's former assistant) Walter Sickert (1860–1942).

Art world liberty ended each day at 4.30 p.m. for Vanessa Stephen when she was obliged to return home to serve tea to her ailing father and his visitors. His death in 1904 was a crucial moment in Vanessa's life and art, as it brought her the opportunity of independence, made manifest by the simple act of moving house.

Gordon Square

The Stephen siblings moved to 46 Gordon Square, a larger, lighter home in less fashionable Bloomsbury. More important than bricks and mortar, however, was the absence of a patriarchal figure and distance from their extended family, and the accompanying freedom to live as they wanted:

> It seemed as if in every way we were making a new beginning in the tall, clean, rather frigid rooms … It was exhilarating to have left the house in which had been so much gloom and depression, to have come to these white walls, large windows opening on to trees and lawns, to have one's own room, be master of one's own time.[11]

The homewares that the family brought with them from Hyde Park Gate, including Julia Margaret Cameron photographs of their mother (**fig. 2**) and a ceramic dish (3), were transformed by the move into the radically different environment of this brighter, less cluttered home. She converted one room into a painting studio, and conceived of the house as a place for living, working and socializing.

Hospitality and sociability were at the heart of the Bloomsbury lifestyle. The Stephens hosted regular Thursday evening 'at homes' attended by people – predominantly Cambridge University classmates of Thoby's – who became lifelong friends: Clive Bell, Leonard Woolf (1880–1969), Lytton Strachey (1880–1932) and John Maynard Keynes (1883–1946). This milieu brought into the home of the Stephen sisters the academic life of a university that did not yet award degrees to women. Many of these friends took rooms in Bloomsbury, ensuring that their circle would become synonymous with this area of London.

Vanessa Stephen's participation in creative and intellectual life was not restricted to her own home. In 1904 she briefly attended the nearby Slade School of Art, which offered women and men art education on equal terms, and where she met many artists of her generation. That year, returning from Italy, she spent time in Paris with Clive Bell, with whom she visited artists' studios and avant-garde exhibitions. Aware of the comparative lack of opportunities for young artists to show modern work in London, Vanessa Stephen founded the Friday Club, an idea she first mentioned to Clive. In addition to an annual exhibition, this club arranged talks and dances so its members could socialize. The membership did not subscribe to a single artistic style, and was drawn mostly from the Royal Academy Schools and the Slade. Among them was the painter Duncan Grant, who had trained in Paris as well as at the Slade, and was already connected to Bloomsbury through his cousin Lytton Strachey. Vanessa was an ardent admirer of Duncan's painting, and the pair would become lifelong artistic collaborators, friends and sometime lovers, a relationship Virginia would later dub a 'left-handed marriage'.[12] Vanessa Stephen married Clive Bell in February 1907, having declined his first proposal in 1905.

At a time when Britain's art institutions rejected the work of young, avant-garde artists, independently organized exhibitions played an important role in introducing new work to the British public. Bell continued to show with the Friday Club until 1913, but her creation continued on without her until 1922 (**fig. 3**). She also participated in other groups and shows, such as the Allied Artists Association, created by critic and suffragist Frank Rutter (1876–1937), and the New English Art Club. Exhibiting *Iceland Poppies* (2) at the latter in 1909, Bell received the encouragement of Walter Sickert, who told her to 'Continuez!' She was, however, excluded from the artist groups around Sickert, the Camden Town and the Fitzroy Street groups, who, overtly or otherwise, did not accept women.

The most impactful exhibition of this period was *Manet and the Post-Impressionists*, which ran from November 1910 to January 1911 at the Grafton Gallery in London. It prominently featured French

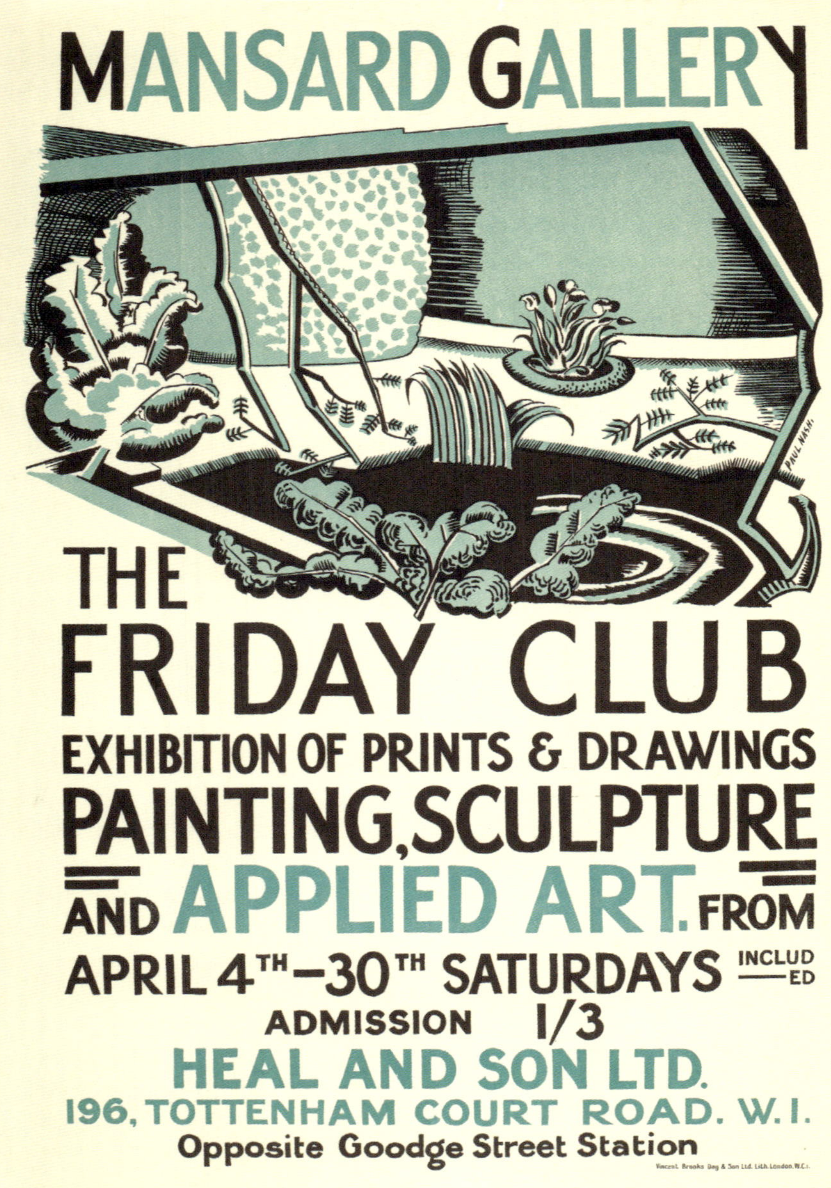
MANSARD GALLERY
PAUL NASH
THE
FRIDAY CLUB
EXHIBITION OF PRINTS & DRAWINGS
PAINTING, SCULPTURE
AND APPLIED ART. FROM
APRIL 4TH – 30TH SATURDAYS INCLUDED
ADMISSION 1/3
HEAL AND SON LTD.
196, TOTTENHAM COURT ROAD. W.1.
Opposite Goodge Street Station
Vincent Brooks Day & Son Ltd. Lith. London. W.C.1.

painter Édouard Manet (1832–1883) and a younger generation of artists almost unknown in Britain: Paul Cezanne (1839–1906), Paul Gauguin (1848–1903), Vincent van Gogh (1853–1890), Georges Seurat (1859–1891), Henri Matisse (1869–1954), André Derain (1880–1954) and Pablo Picasso (1881–1973). The phrase 'post-Impressionism' to describe these painters was coined by the exhibition's organizer, the artist, critic and curator Roger Fry, who had recently returned to Britain after a spell working at the Metropolitan Museum of Art in New York. The honorary committee of *Manet and the Post-Impressionists* featured Bloomsbury group members, including Clive Bell. The show opened to a tirade of critical abuse, but this attracted 25,000 paying visitors who wished to know what all the fuss was about. Vanessa Bell described its transformative influence on artists in Britain, stating: 'here was a sudden pointing to a possible path, a sudden liberation and encouragement to feel for oneself which were absolutely overwhelming'.[13] Her sister saw a more profound effect, stating 'On or around December 1910, human character changed.'[14]

Vanessa Bell became increasingly interested in Fry's artistic theories and the artists he championed, and they started an affair in 1911. The following year, Fry curated the *Second Post-Impressionist Exhibition*. The couple's intimacy is apparent not only in their erotically charged correspondence but in a painting of the large gallery of this landmark exhibition (fig. 4) thought to be by Fry but sometimes attributed to Bell. It shows the Matisse room of the exhibition that featured *Le Luxe II* (1907–8) (32) and *The Red Studio* (1911). Alongside Matisse, Derain, Picasso and the French painter Pierre Bonnard (1867–1947), whose highly coloured domestic scenes would have appealed to Bell, the 1912 exhibition featured her own work among that of other British and Russian artists. Bell was one of five women artists, and exhibited four paintings, two of which were probably interiors.[15] Even though Clive Bell wrote the catalogue's introductory essay on the British artists, he did not mention his wife by name. Vanessa Bell also had the idea for a poster design

Fig. 3 Paul Nash, poster for *Friday Club* exhibition, 1921
Colour lithograph, 76.3 × 51 cm
Victoria and Albert Museum, London
(V&A: E.238-1980)

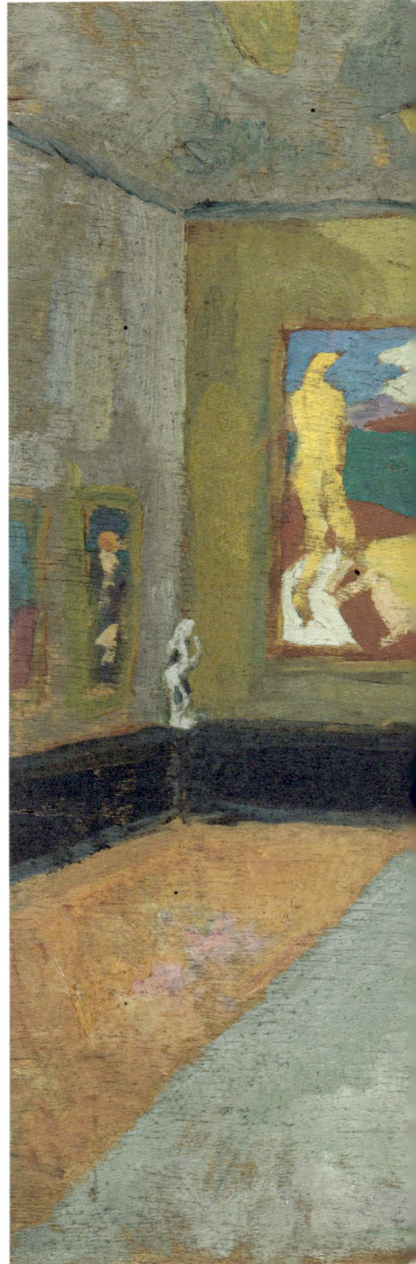

Fig. 4 Roger Fry, *A Room of the Second Post-Impressionist Exhibition in London at the Grafton Galleries*, 1912
Oil on canvas, 50.5 × 60.5 cm
Musée d'Orsay, Paris
(RF 1977 179)

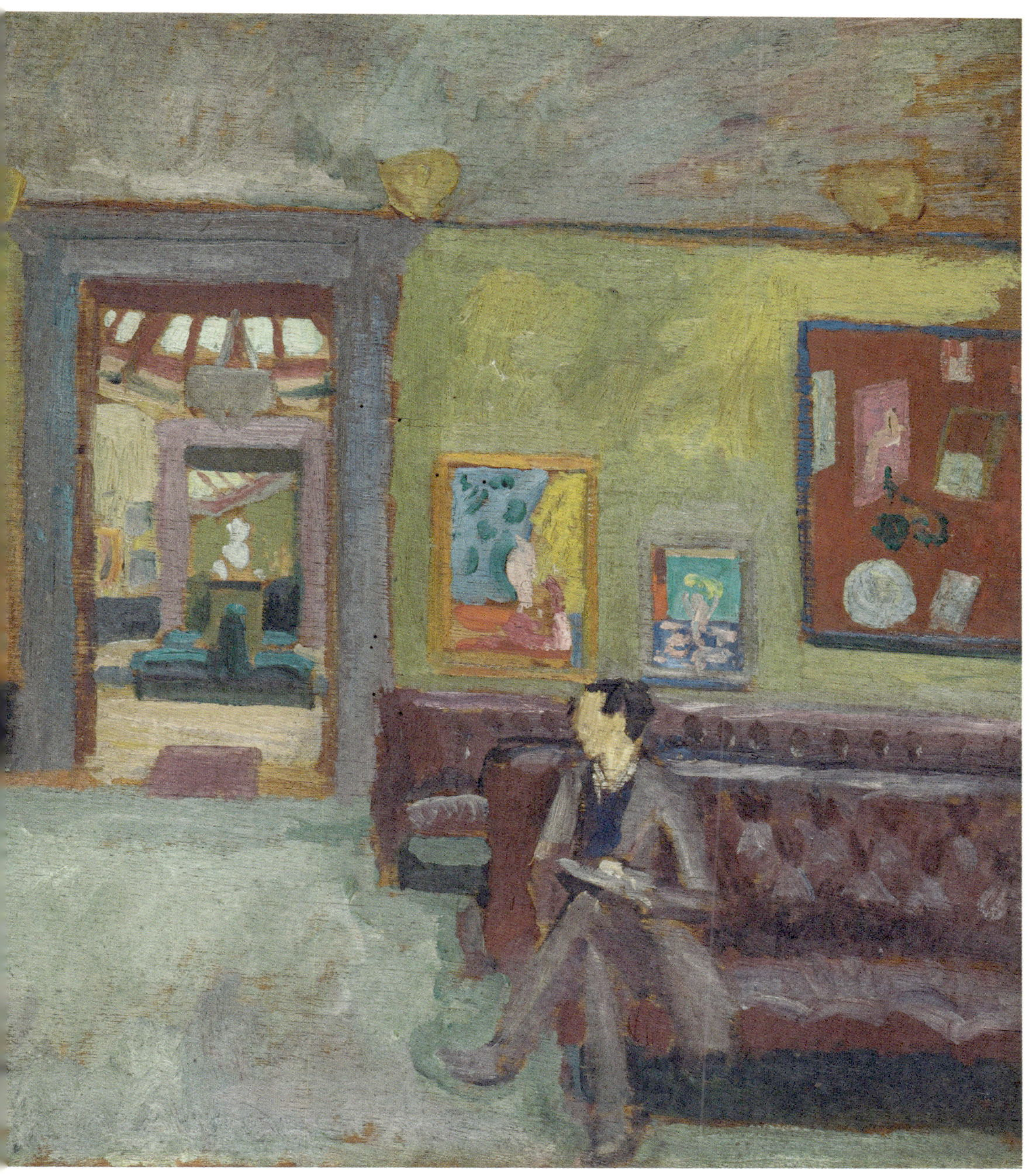

showing a woman with a hand raised in horror, which was drawn by Duncan Grant in a Cubist-inspired angular style (fig. 5).[16]

Bell's central role within the modern British art scene was confirmed in 1913, when she became co-director of Omega Workshops Ltd. This company was founded by Fry, with Grant as the other co-director, and had its workshop and showroom at 33 Fitzroy Square, half a mile from Bell's Bloomsbury home. The Workshops' aim was to bring post-Impressionism to interior design and homewares, an aspiration the trio had already begun with their designs at Fry's home, Durbins, near Guildford, south-west of London. Their clientele boasted the more avant-garde members of British society.

Omega was a collective undertaking that initially employed numerous artists – many of whom were members of the Friday Club – providing them with much-needed income, including Henri Doucet (1883–1915), Frederick and Jessie Etchells (1886–1973; 1892–1933), Henri Gaudier-Brzeska (1891–1915), Winifred Gill (1891–1981), Nina Hamnett (1890–1956), Wyndham Lewis (1882–1957), Paul Nash (1889–1946) and Edward Wadsworth (1889–1949). Rather than signing their work, artists marked products with Ω (omega), the final letter of the Greek alphabet, suggesting that their creations were the last word in design.

With Omega colleagues, Bell collaborated on whole room arrangements, including a model nursery (11) and a room for the 1913 Ideal Home Exhibition. She decorated screens, panels and ceramics with the curvaceous stylized forms and vivid colour palettes favoured by the Fauvism of Derain and Matisse. She also created Cubist-influenced geometrical designs for rugs, lamps, furnishing fabrics – and, from 1915, dresses – some of which were made by professional manufacturers, with others copied in-house by Omega assistants. Bell's experience of producing stark, simple designs led her painting style into abstraction. She continued to make figurative paintings, especially still lifes, which sometimes featured her textiles and other Omega products. She exhibited her

Fig. 5 Duncan Grant, poster for *Second Post-Impressionist Exhibition*, 1912
Line block print, 85.6 × 57.6 cm
Victoria and Albert Museum, London
(V&A: E.737-1955)
Given by Miss Margery Fry, J.P.

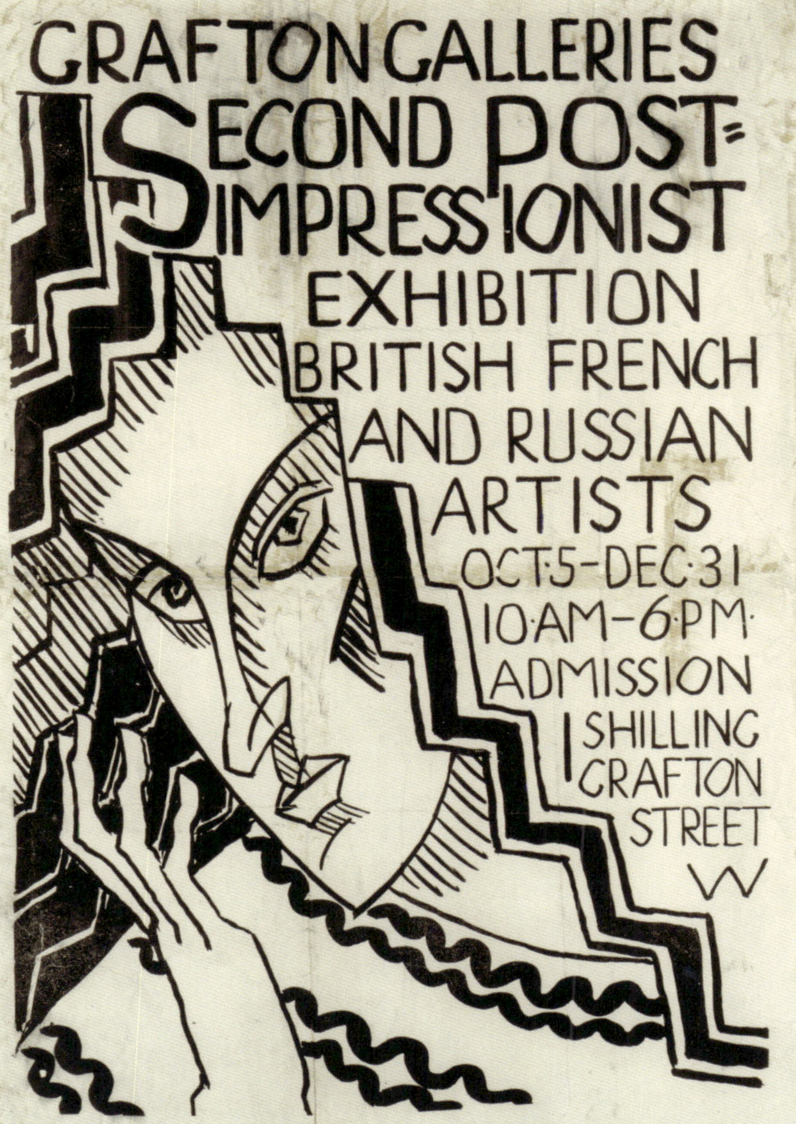
GRAFTON GALLERIES
SECOND POST=
IMPRESSIONIST
EXHIBITION
BRITISH FRENCH
AND RUSSIAN
ARTISTS
OCT·5–DEC·31
10·AM–6·PM·
ADMISSION
1 SHILLING
GRAFTON
STREET
W

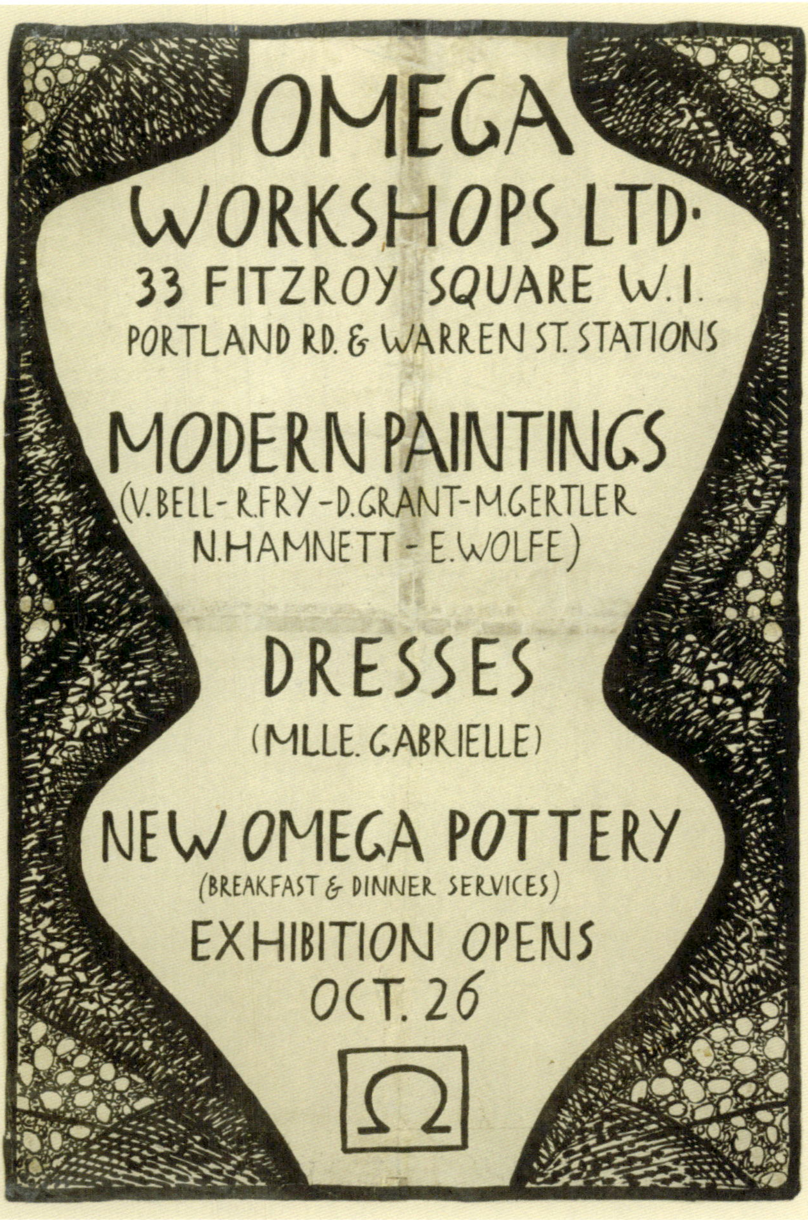
OMEGA
WORKSHOPS LTD.
33 FITZROY SQUARE W.I.
PORTLAND RD. & WARREN ST. STATIONS
MODERN PAINTINGS
(V.BELL - R.FRY - D.GRANT - M.GERTLER
N.HAMNETT - E.WOLFE)
DRESSES
(MLLE. GABRIELLE)
NEW OMEGA POTTERY
(BREAKFAST & DINNER SERVICES)
EXHIBITION OPENS
OCT. 26
Ω

paintings alongside those by Fry, Grant, Hamnett and others, and Omega homewares, at the Workshops' regular exhibitions, including in 1918 (**fig. 6**), the year before the company wound down.

Creating Omega designs came naturally to Bell, who had been decorating her home for a decade. From its vermillion front door to the studio walls, the Omega aesthetic owed much to 46 Gordon Square; likewise, the Workshops' fluidity between decorative, domestic schemes and easel paintings owed much to Bell. This was not, however, amenable to all her artist friends. Grant remembered 'Sickert coming to see Vanessa in Gordon Square once, when we had painted the end of the wall, and he was *furious.* "You might be painting pictures!"'[17]

Charleston

The move to Bloomsbury marked Bell's first break with domestic convention. The second was her setting up home in the country. First she rented Asheham House in Sussex with her sister, then lived in Wissett Lodge in Suffolk with Grant, before moving into Charleston Farmhouse, also in Sussex, in 1916, where she would live on and off for the rest of her life. Putting distance between herself and London society emboldened her sense of liberation from Edwardian propriety. Staying at Asheham, she exchanged her London clothes for looser, more comfortable attire; and from Wissett Lodge she wrote to Fry that 'I feel such a savage here as if I could never go to a tea party again.'[18]

Social life on her own terms was crucial to Bell's country homes. Grant was ever-present, and both cohabitating and painting side by side further fostered their relationship. Invitations were regularly issued to the Bloomsbury group to join them for weekends or longer periods. She insisted upon informality and both her arrangement of her homes and her manner made her guests feel at ease.

With the outbreak of the First World War in 1914, Bell had to find her family a more permanent residence away from London.

Fig. 6 Omega Workshops Ltd advertisement, 1918
Lithograph, 76.2 × 50.6 cm
Victoria and Albert Museum, London
(V&A: E.738-1955)

By now mother to two young sons, Julian and Quentin, Bell's relationship with her husband, Clive, was increasingly distant, her affair with Fry was over and her love for Grant readily apparent. All three men were, like Bell, pacifists, but only Grant was eligible for military conscription (Fry being too old, and Clive Bell's situation being complicated by earlier injury).[19] Vanessa Bell found Grant and his lover, the writer David 'Bunny' Garnett (1892–1981), work as farm labourers near Lewes in Sussex. It was not far from Asheham, where Virginia and Leonard Woolf – married in 1912 – were living. Leonard found a nearby farmhouse that the Woolfs suggested Bell rent for her, the children, Grant and Garnett. In this ménage à trois, Bell created a place of safety for her community of conscientious objectors during wartime, and also for same-sex relationships when homosexuality was illegal in Britain and the subject of increased scandal following the trial of Oscar Wilde in 1895. Bell's belief that prejudice against homosexuality was analogous with that against post-Impressionist painting – expressed in a letter to Grant in 1914 – underlines how her progressive social and aesthetic views were connected.

Bell would make Charleston a thoroughly modern home for the Bloomsbury group. When first visiting, Bell noted that the three-storey farmhouse had a large garden with fruit trees and a beehive, and large, light rooms. Renting an unfurnished house, Bell hoped 'to carry out the idea I have always had of bedrooms with the minimum of furniture'.[20] While their ambitions were modern, the conveniences of the house, which dated back to the seventeenth century, with some later alterations, were not. Charleston had no telephone, electricity, central heating or hot water; cold water had to be hand-pumped. Reaching the house required a long walk over farm tracks from the closest train station at Glynde. Life at Charleston was, however, made more comfortable by the employ of a nurse for the children, a housemaid and a cook.

As the war raged, Bell and Grant began decorating Charleston. Reflecting on this in 1921, Bell wrote, 'I am rather astonished on coming here again to find how much energy we spent on this place, how many tables and chairs and doors we painted and how many colour schemes we invented, considering what a struggle it was to exist here at all.'[21] The style, and the palette of vibrant colour against a neutral grey ground, reflected their painting practices and their ongoing involvement with the Omega Workshops. Having obtained the landlord's permission, they disguised the existing wallpaper with a wash of distemper. Bell and Grant decorated each other's bedrooms and their artistic intimacy soon led to the conception of their child, Angelica, born at Charleston on Christmas Day 1918.

The blurring of boundaries between Charleston as studio, subject and surface, as well as family home and social hub, is exemplified by *The Tub* (33). Bell made this painting, picturing the Charleston sitting room with pond in the background, in her first-floor studio in 1917, and planned to hang it in the Garden Room. The model is Mary Hutchinson (1889–1977), a friend of Bell's and frequent guest at her houses, a client of Omega and the lover of Clive Bell.

After the war Charleston became a weekend and summer residence, one conveniently close to Virginia and Leonard Woolf's new Sussex home, Monk's House. Bell returned to Bloomsbury, living in multiple addresses in Gordon Square and taking a studio, alongside Grant, at 8 Fitzroy Street. The Bloomsbury group were once again able to travel internationally. Bell and her family spent time in Italy, and she regularly visited friends' French homes, including those of artists Ethel Sands (1873–1962) and Anna Hope Hudson (1869–1957) at the Château d'Auppegard near Dieppe in Normandy, and painter Simon Bussy (1870–1954) and novelist Dorothy Strachey (Lytton's sister; 1865–1960) at Le Souco, in Roquebrune, near Monaco. In 1927, on one of her regular visits to Provence in the south of France, a landscape made famous by Cezanne, Bell discovered a disused farmworkers' house in Cassis called La Bergère, which she had renovated and used for painting trips.

Charleston, and especially its garden, remained an important Bloomsbury meeting place. Wild when they moved in, the garden was laid out by Roger Fry during the war. It is seen in many of the painted and photographic portraits of the family and wider members of the Bloomsbury group. Bell had been photographing her family and friends for decades, capturing candid, carefree shots in the garden, in stark contrast to the formal studio photography of her childhood family albums. In one example from 1928 (**fig. 7**), a jovial group, featuring Quentin and Julian Bell, Duncan Grant and Clive Bell sandwiched between authors Frances Partridge (1900–2004) and Beatrice Mayor (1885–1971) with Roger Fry and another writer, Raymond Mortimer (1895–1980), in the foreground, are gathered around a sculpted bust with a wine bottle for a head, topped with Vanessa's own hat, standing in for the artist herself. The flowerbeds, later tended by a gardener, also provided Bell with numerous varieties of flowers to paint and incorporate into her designs. The kitchen garden towards the rear, and the multiple apple trees and fruit bushes, also supplied the family with provisions that would be increasingly essential when the outbreak of the Second World War brought Bell, her family and friends back to Charleston full-time.

The group would be different from that which had gathered during the last war; Bloomsbury had lost Lytton Strachey in 1932 and Roger Fry two years later. As the rise of fascism across Europe brought mass bloodshed and tragedy, Bell experienced tragic losses on a personal level with the death of her son Julian in the Spanish Civil War in 1937, then that of her sister Virginia Woolf in 1941.

From 1939 Bell not only made changes to the house to accommodate its evolving residents but also produced a series of paintings showing them safely ensconced in their shared home (**45, 47, 49**). Bell and her family decorated the house and her children's artistic talents were put to work. Charleston entered a new chapter with the arrival of Bell's grandchildren. In 1942 Angelica married David Garnett and, the following year, their daughter Amaryllis was born. As she had done with her own children, Bell drew and painted her many grandchildren who, as they grew, were paid to model in their grandparents' studios.

Fig. 7 Photograph of family and friends taken by Vanessa Bell in the walled garden of her home, Charleston Farmhouse, Sussex, 1928
Tate

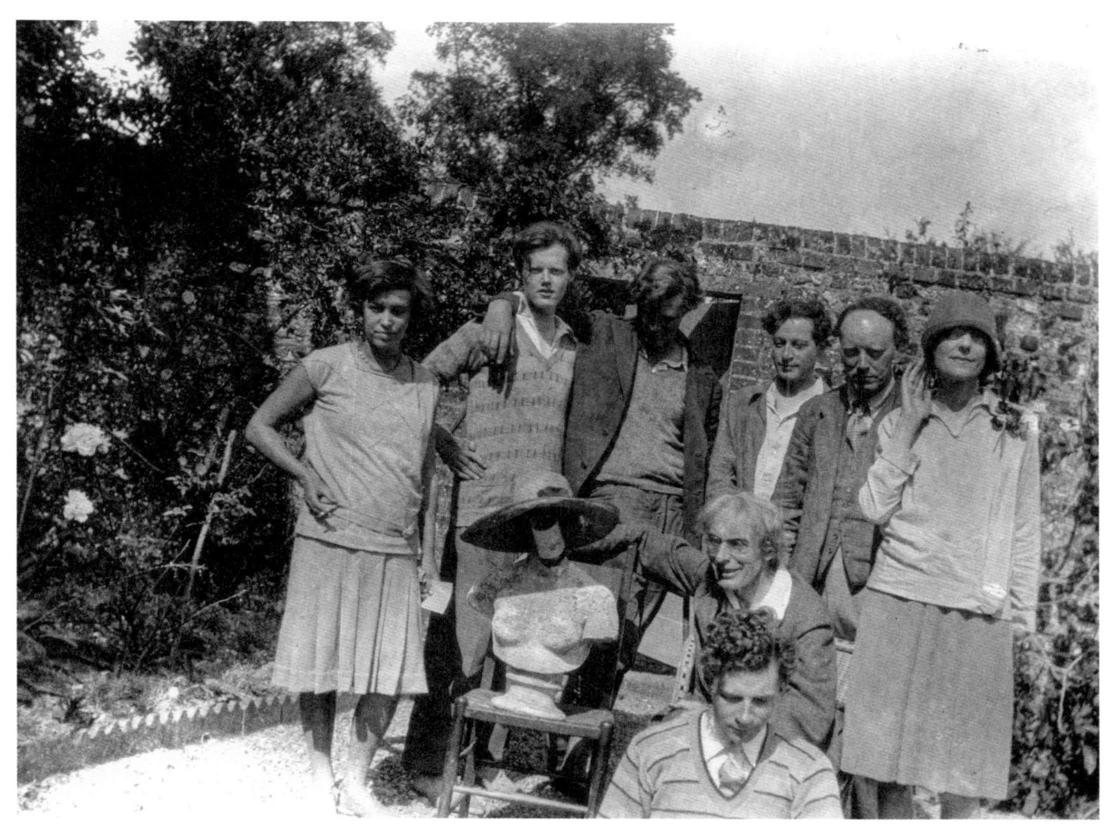

Other Rooms

While Bell's homes continued to serve as preferred studio and subject, her work was not limited to her own domestic sphere. She exhibited in London with the Lefevre and Leicester galleries, both pioneering commercial modern art galleries, as well as with the London Group and the London Artists' Association, both artist-led organizations in which she played active roles. Bell continued to decorate interiors, a profession that had long been seen as women's work, but became fashionably so in interwar London.[22] A 1925 advertisement for Bell and Grant's company gave her (perhaps alphabetical) top billing:

> VANESSA BELL
> DUNCAN GRANT
> DECORATIONS
> THEATRE . HOUSE . FURNITURE
> ETCETERA
> 8, FITZROY STREET, W.1[23]

This enterprise started close to home with their redecoration of 46 Gordon Square after John Maynard Keynes took over the lease in 1918 and made Bell's former home his London residence. Keynes, by now an influential economist working for the government, also had rooms at King's College Cambridge, for which Bell and Grant created eight paintings of personifications of the Arts and Sciences in 1920, covering a mural Grant had painted 10 years previously.

Some of Bell and Grant's clients were carried over from the Omega period. When, in 1926, Mary Hutchinson moved out of River House in Hammersmith, which Bell and Grant had decorated a decade earlier, she commissioned the pair to design and paint the interiors of her new home at Albert Gate, near Regent's Park. Both Hutchinson residences were featured in *Vogue* magazine, where Bell and Grant's decorative schemes were regularly illustrated through the mid-1920s. An article from November 1924 dedicated to the pair extolled: 'They can turn their versatile hands to anything, from the complete scheme of decoration down to the last detail of a drawing-room, to the painting of a bowl, a tile, a screen or a cushion, the designing of a carpet or a chair-cover.'[24]

The role of painters like Bell and Grant in interior design, especially in Britain, was noted in the book *The New Interior Decoration: An Introduction to its Principles, and International Survey of its Methods* written by former *Vogue* editor Dorothy Todd (1883–1966) and Raymond Mortimer in 1929. Both had Bloomsbury connections, which might explain Bell and Grant's substantial inclusion amid the more minimalist, functional designs of architects Le Corbusier (1887–1965) and Marcel Breuer (1902–1981) found on its pages. The Music Room (**63**) that Bell and Grant designed for the Lefevre Gallery was also featured, in colour, in Derek Patmore's *Colour Schemes for the Modern Home* (1933). Again, the whimsical Bloomsbury aesthetic contrasted with interior designer Syrie Maugham's (1879–1955) monochrome and mirrors, favoured by the new generation of Bright Young Things centred around photographer Cecil Beaton (1904–1980).

The photographic attention paid to Bell and Grant's decorative works in the 1920s has created a valuable record of those that do not survive in situ. Mortimer's own apartment, decorated by Bell and Grant in 1925, was disassembled, and its panels are now in the V&A. The home of Virginia and Leonard Woolf at Tavistock Square was, like Bell's own studio, destroyed in the Second World War. Colour photographs of Woolf at home taken in 1939 by Gisèle Freund (1908–2000; **fig. 9**) record the palette of the decorations that *Vogue* could only describe, and capture Woolf within an environment that would soon be lost. Bell's theatrical set for the ballet *High Yellow* (1932) survives only as a design. Other Bell designs went unrealized, such as her submission to a design competition in the *Architectural Review* – awarded third prize – and her initial design for a commission for a panel aboard RMS *Queen Mary*, which was rejected by the Roman Catholic authorities for being offensive. While her public

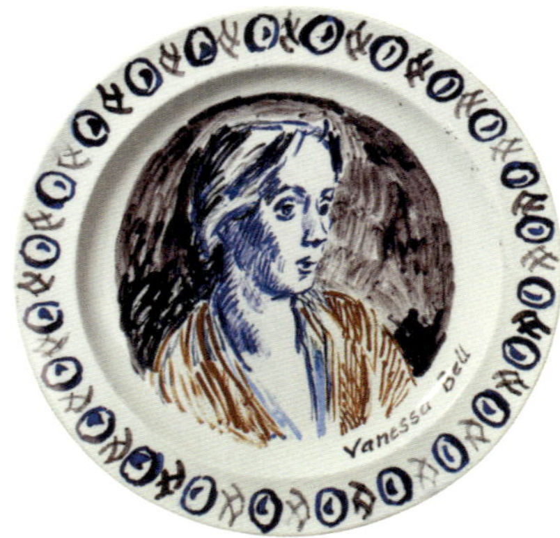

Fig. 8 Duncan Grant, portrait of Vanessa Bell, 1932–3
Hand-painted on a Wedgwood blank earthenware plate
Charleston
(CHA/P/708)

Fig. 9 Gisèle Freund, *Virginia Woolf*, 1939
Gelatin silver print, 24.1 × 18 cm
Victoria and Albert Museum, London
(V&A: E.88-2003)
Given by John and Judith Hillelson

commissions were few, she did create tile panels for the Garden Hostel student accommodation at King's College, Cambridge; serve on the Edwin Austin Abbey Memorial Trust Fund for Mural Painting, commissioning modern artists to paint public buildings; and decorate the small Sussex church of St Michael and All Angels in Berwick with Grant and Quentin Bell.

Charleston is today unique among Bell and Grant's complete domestic decorative schemes, but Bell's furnishings and homewares, designed on her own and with Grant, have survived. The recent rediscovery of the hand-painted dinner service featuring famous women that Bell and Grant made for museum director Kenneth Clark (1903–1983) has initiated renewed interest in Bell's work as a designer, and as a famous woman herself (**fig. 8**).

While this commission was overtly exclusive, this was not the case for all of Bell's production. A vogue in the 1930s for bringing the work of modern British artists into middle-class homes meant that Bell was one of a generation of painters commissioned to design for manufacturers, namely ceramics for Arthur J. Wilkinson & Co. Ltd and fabrics for Allan Walton Textiles. The same egalitarian attitude is found in her production of prints for the Artists

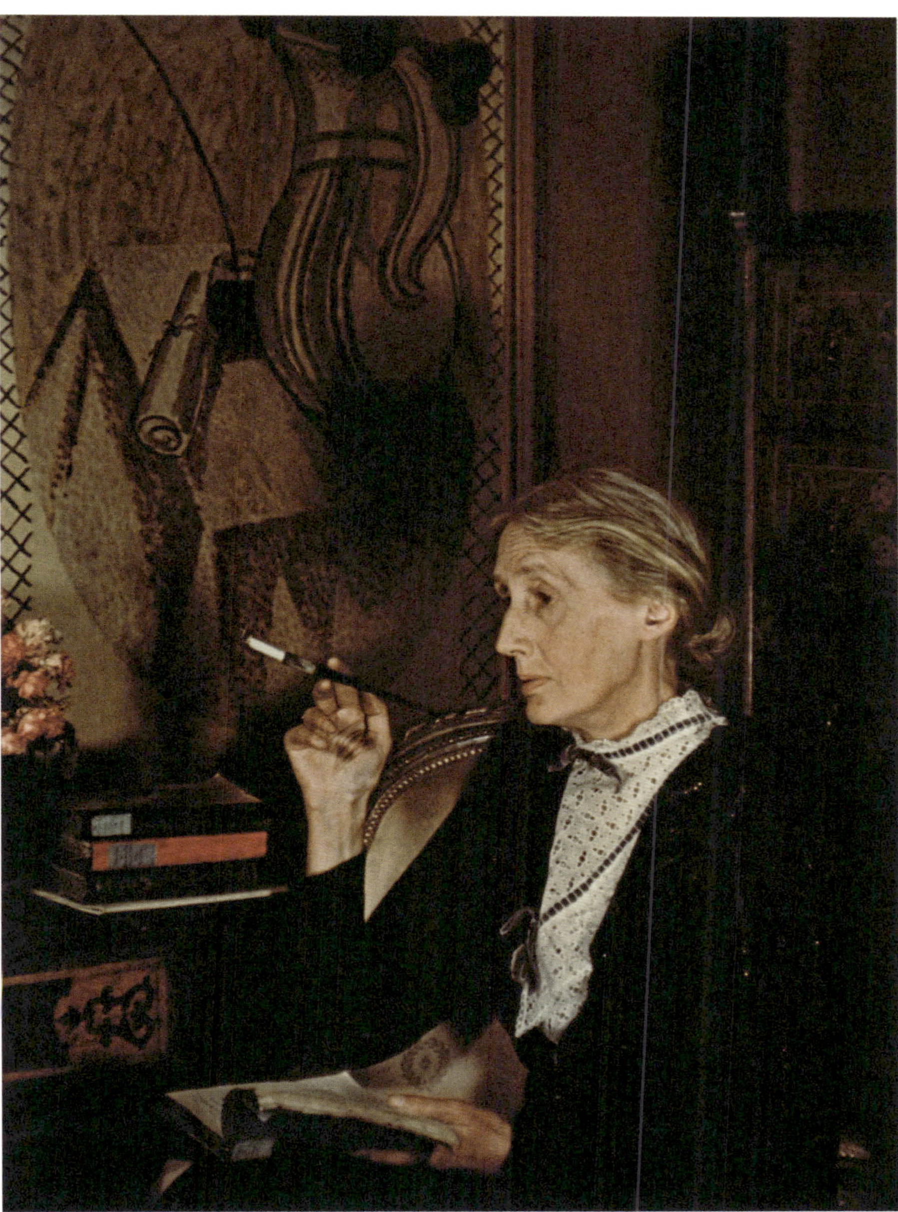

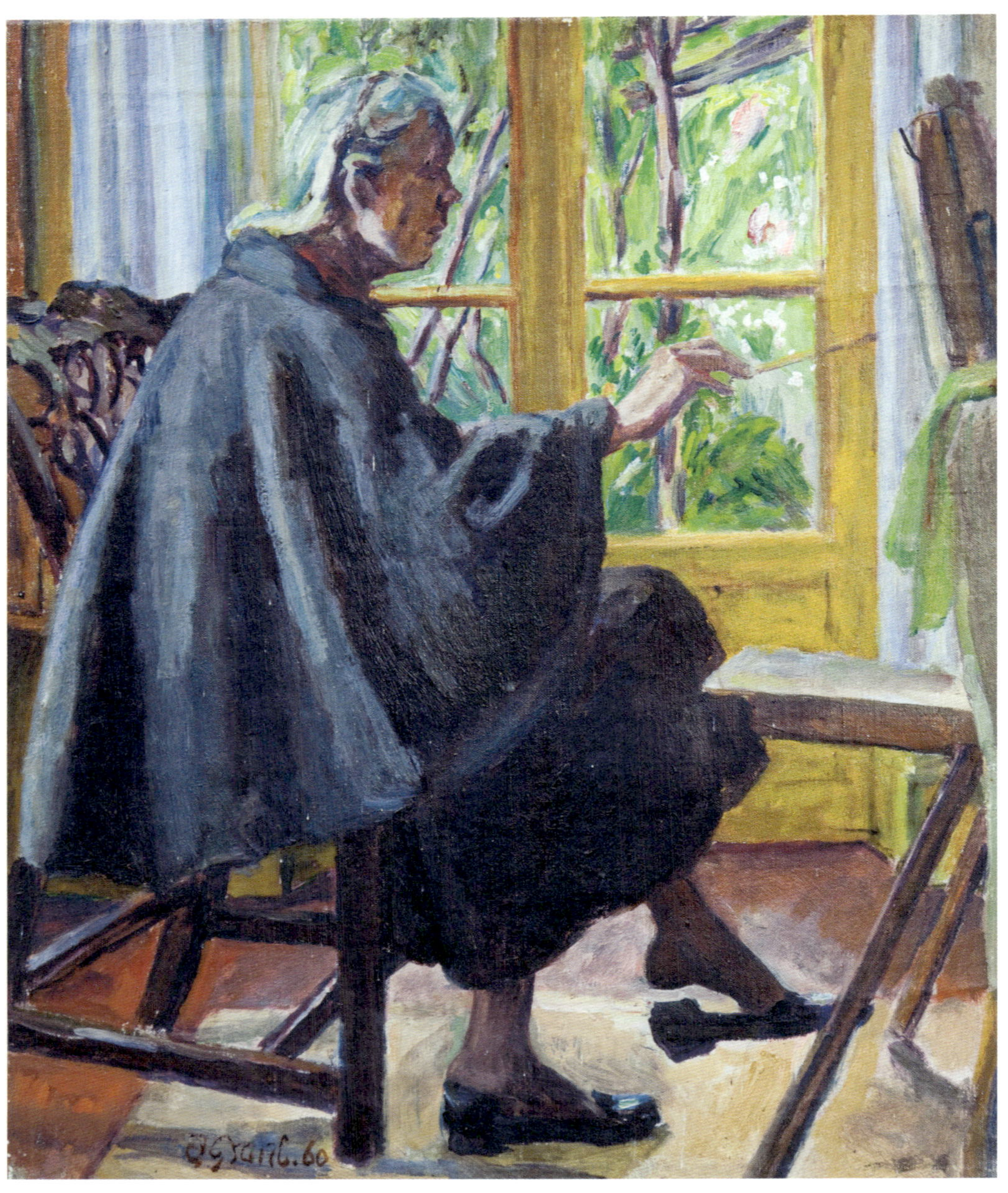
D.Grant.60

International Association, Contemporary Lithographs and Miller's Press, all of which sought to make modern prints more accessible.

Perhaps the greatest vehicle for bringing Bell's work into strangers' homes on a grand scale were the covers that she designed for the Hogarth Press. Virginia and Leonard Woolf founded this publishing house in 1917 and named it after their Richmond home, Hogarth House. Virginia Woolf was anxious for this enterprise not to be considered a 'home-made hobby', so her sister as cover artist may not have been the most obvious choice.[25] Nor were Bell's book jackets popular with booksellers or critics. Yet, from *Kew Gardens* in 1919 (**79**), over which the sisters quarrelled about the poor quality of the printing of Bell's woodcuts, through all Woolf's novels bar two, to posthumously published essay collections such as *The Death of the Moth* (**86**), this collaboration cemented the sisters' artistic relationship during and beyond their lifetimes.

One of the last images of Vanessa Bell, painted by Duncan Grant in 1960, the year before she died, makes clear her lifelong commitment to her art (**fig. 10**). The painting shows Bell, aged 81, at work in an interior, in front of French windows leading to a garden. Today it hangs at Charleston, but Bell is not seen at home, but visiting Le Souco, the home of Simon Bussy and Dorothy Strachey. Bell sits at an easel, painting an unseen picture, her brush poised centimetres from the canvas, almost invisible against the yellow windows framing her profile. She wears a voluminous black smock that disguises most of the chair beneath her, and her left shoe hangs off her foot.

This intimately observed portrait of Bell reiterates the fact that the homes of so many in the Bloomsbury circle, as well as her own, became the subjects, studios and surfaces for her painting, in turn testimony to how her radical social impulses went hand in hand with her radical approach to art and design. To look at Vanessa Bell through the modern rooms she painted and created, and the modern life she enabled within them, is to see how holistically she interpreted the central tenet of modernism: to blend art and life.

Fig. 10 Duncan Grant,
Vanessa Bell Painting at Le Souco, 1960
Oil on canvas, 46 × 38 cm
Charleston
(CHA/P/103)

Plates

This cool-toned still life of a vivid green medicine bottle, a small grey-white bowl and a lidded urn – reputed to be a pharmacy jar – is named after the white and red poppies that lie across the foreground. Bell rejected narratives within paintings, but her subject's medicinal (even poisonous and narcotic) qualities and her use of trios has encouraged biographical readings of a picture made during a period of flirtation between her husband and her sister. This rare early painting by Bell shows her attention to composition and skills as a colourist. It survived because it hung at Charleston, where it remains today, as does the jar.

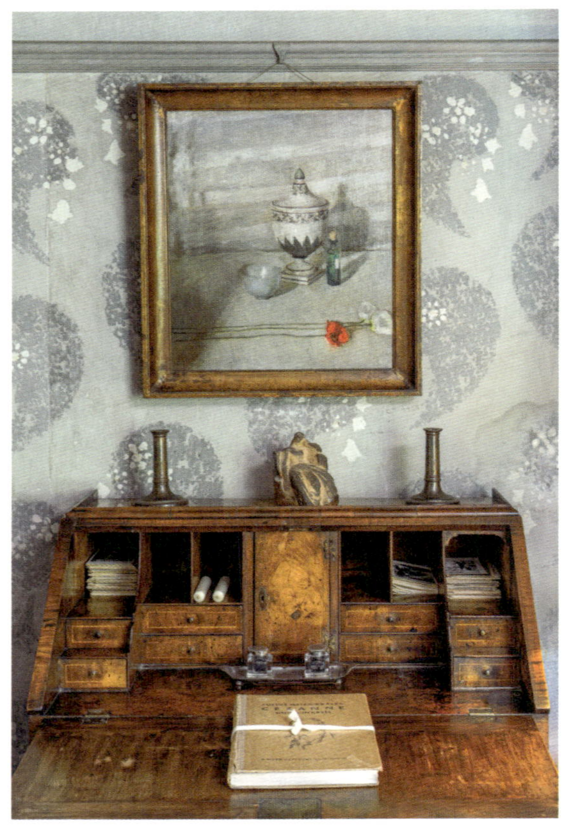

1. *Iceland Poppies* in the Garden Room at Charleston

2. *Iceland Poppies*, *c.* 1908–9
Oil on canvas, 54 × 45 cm
Charleston
(CHA/P/468)

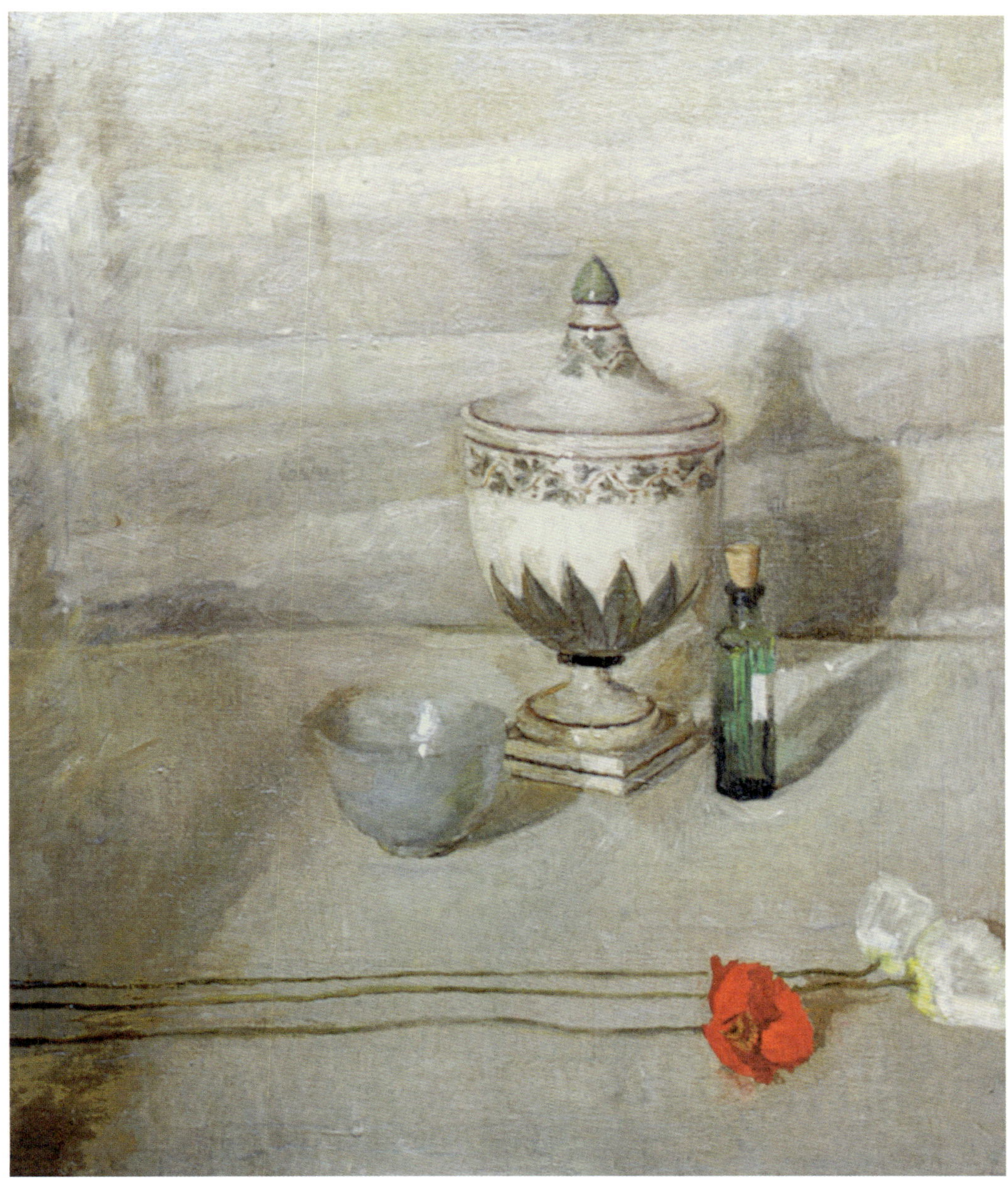

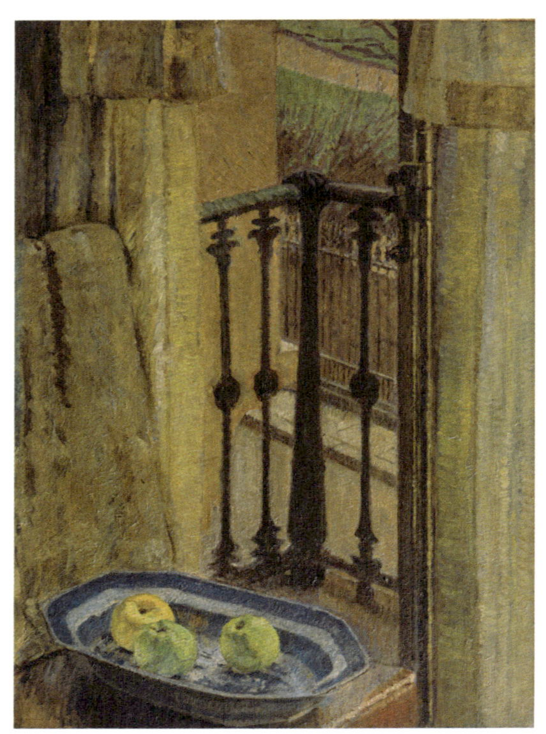

3. *Apples: 46 Gordon Square*, *c.* 1909
Oil on canvas, 71 × 50.8 cm
Charleston
(LL/CHA/P/4)

Windows are a leitmotif in Bell's painting. Here, in her home at 46 Gordon Square, London, the private space of her drawing room collides with the public realm, as wrought-iron balcony meets the railings in the square beneath. The unusual viewpoint and awkward cropping are indebted to the painter Walter Sickert, while the apples in the foreground owe much to Paul Cezanne. They are arranged in a blue-and-white Chinese porcelain dish, which Bell brought to Gordon Square from her childhood home at Hyde Park Gate: an ornamental presence in this otherwise sparse home and composition.

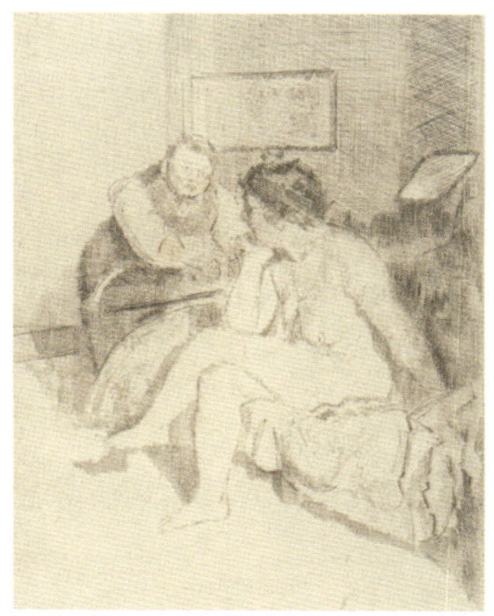

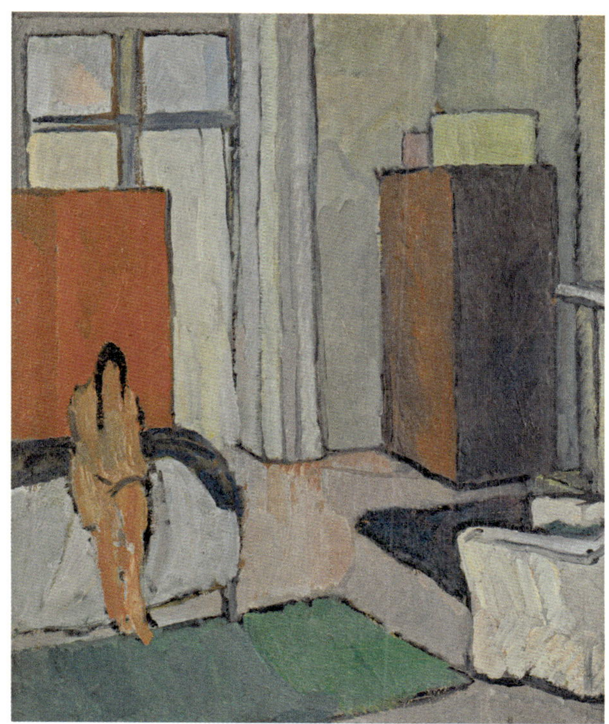

4. Walter Sickert, *Jack Ashore*, *c.* 1911
Etching, 38.3 × 27.6 cm
Victoria and Albert Museum, London
(V&A: CIRC.115-1961)

5. *Bedroom, Gordon Square*, 1912
Oil on canvas, 56.3 × 46.2 cm
Adelaide Art Gallery
(849P29)

This painting shows the stark domestic architecture and simple bedroom furnishings that Bell preferred for her Bloomsbury home. She has distilled these into almost abstract, geometrical forms with thick, dark outlines. The figure of the nude woman seated on the bed gives a sense of intimacy but, as in the overmantel design (**6**) from the same period, she is not sexualized. In fact, she appears quite comfortable, in contrast to scenes of the same subject by Bell's friend and neighbour Walter Sickert (**4**).

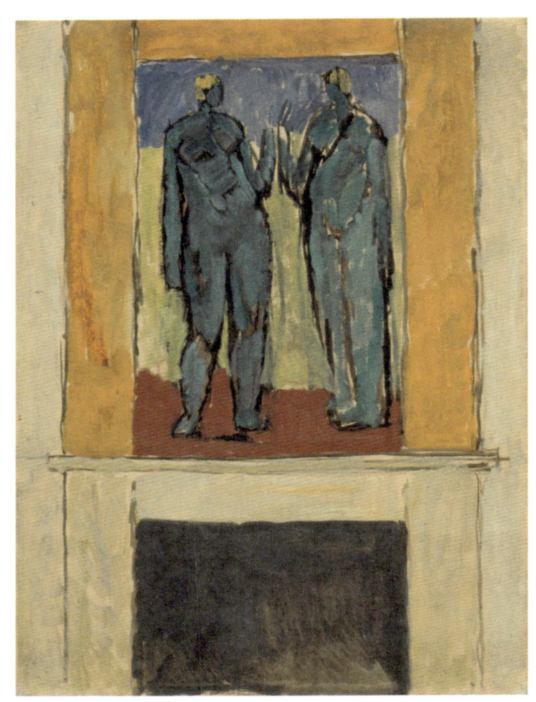

6. Design for an overmantel, 1912–13
Oil on paper, 76.2 × 55.9 cm
Yale Center for British Art
(B1992.14.1)

Fireplaces were often central to Bell's decorative schemes, as the hearth at the heart of the home. This overmantel design features two imposing nudes whose emerald-green forms are similar to those in a screen painted in the same period (13). This was probably an unrealized design for Bell's first-floor studio at 46 Gordon Square, as the few surviving photographs of this room show a different, much larger picture pinned to the wall. This colour design provides insight into her process of decorating her own studio space, and the palette she planned for her London home, which is now only known through black-and-white photography.

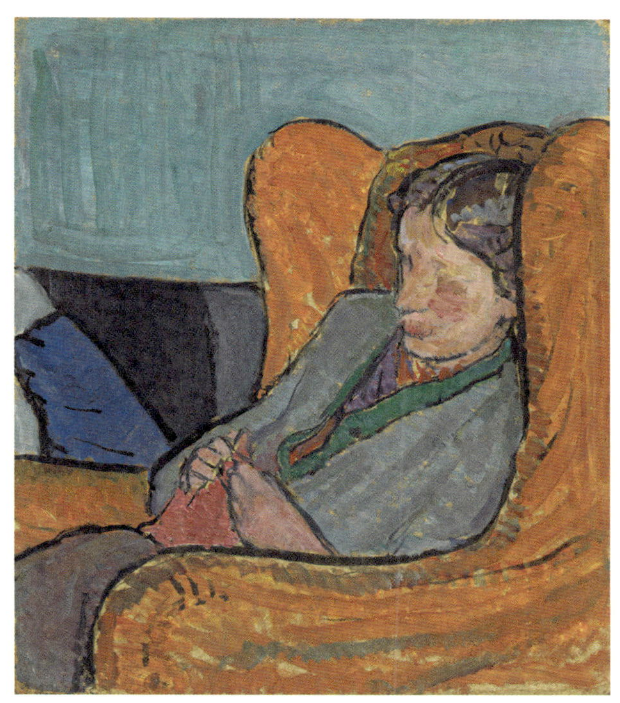

7. *Virginia Woolf*, 1912
Oil on board, 40 × 34 cm
National Portrait Gallery, London
(NPG5933)

This intimate portrait shows the artist's sister seated within touching distance, nestled in an armchair, knitting in hand. It was painted at Asheham, Virginia Woolf's Sussex home from 1912 to 1919 that, for a few years, Bell also shared. As is often the case with Bell's portraiture, especially of close friends and family, the face is indistinct, the features blurred. The armchair, by contrast, is clearly delineated and its bright orange colour and wingback design are recognizable from other paintings of their social circle gathered in this room.

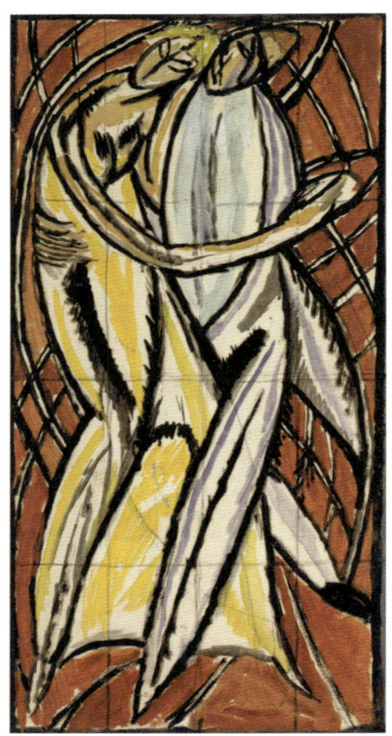

8. *Dancing Couple*, 1913
Gouache and oil on paper, 76.2 × 37.5 cm
Victoria and Albert Museum, London
(V&A: E.734-1955)
Given by Miss Margery Fry, J.P.

This large, squared-up study was made in preparation for an enormous painting on canvas, now lost, for the facade of the Omega Workshops at 33 Fitzroy Square. The pointed elliptical shapes of the stylized figures give a sense of movement and dynamism. Dressed in yellow and blue, their attire reflects the bright palette and relaxed cuts of Omega textiles and clothing. While painting the larger version outside Asheham House in Sussex, Bell included a sketch of this work in a letter to Fry, reporting that their mutual friend 'Marjorie [Strachey] thinks them hideous and we shall be stopped by the police, but I can't see what she means.'[26]

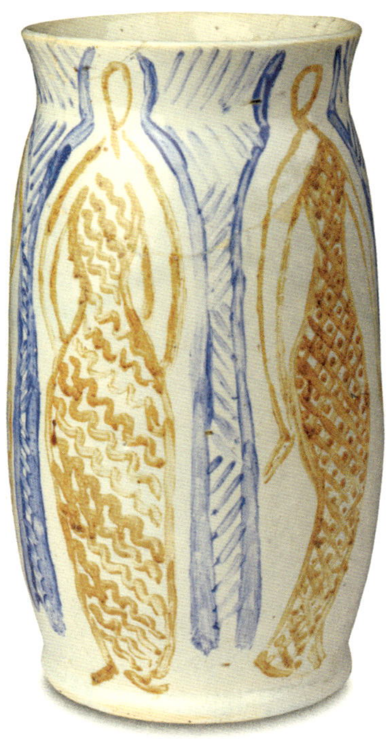

9. Vase, 1914, probably thrown by Roger Fry and painted by Vanessa Bell for Omega Workshops Ltd
Tin-glazed earthenware, painted in blue and ochre
Victoria and Albert Museum, London (V&A: Circ.257-1964)
Given by Miss H. Sollas

While many Omega products remain entirely anonymous, this pot is thought to be a collaboration between Bell and her friend and lover Roger Fry for the Workshops. He made the vase and she painted the simple ochre figures wearing patterned dresses and divided by blue decoration. Fry had learned how to throw pots the previous year so that the Omega Workshops could produce their own ceramics, rather than decorating industrially produced wares. In the Omega catalogue Fry wrote: 'Pottery is essentially a form of sculpture, and its surface should express directly the artist's sensibility both of proportion and surface.'[27]

Collaboration was central to the Omega Workshops, and their products were made by many hands and deliberately signed with an Ω instead of an artist's name. These hand-painted wooden lampstands favoured geometric, Cubist-inspired designs and bold colour schemes, but did not seek to emulate the neatness of industrial production. Bell was one of the many artists who painted lampstands and shades; some of her popular designs for shades, remembered by Omega artist Winifred Gill as featuring straight lines and 'three shades of chrome yellow, with a background of deep blue and purple', were copied by others in the workshop.[28]

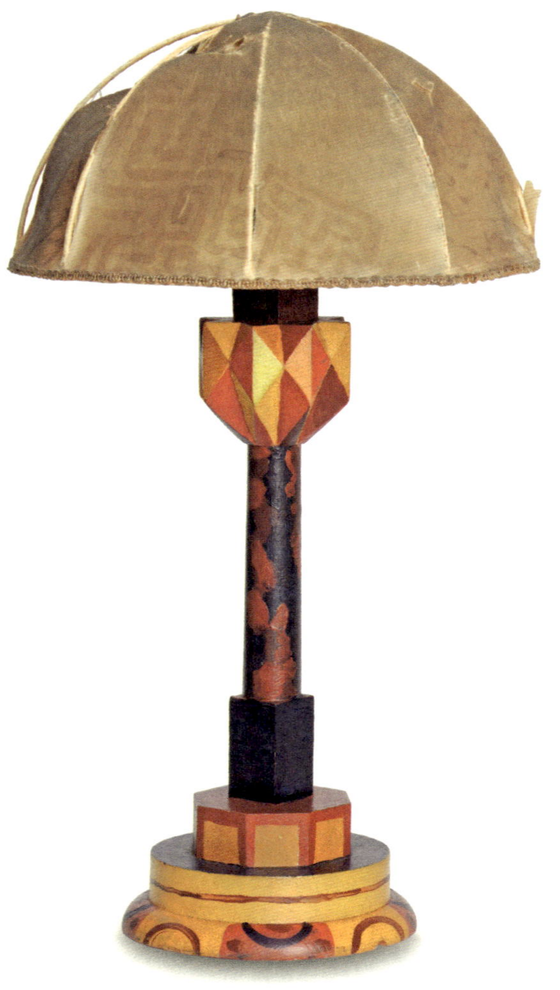

10. Lampstands, 1913–19, made by Omega Workshops Ltd
Turned, carved and painted wood
Victoria and Albert Museum, London
(V&A: Misc.2:17-1934, Misc.2:16-1934, Misc.2:15/1&2-1934)
Given by Mrs Margaret H. Armitage (née Bulley)

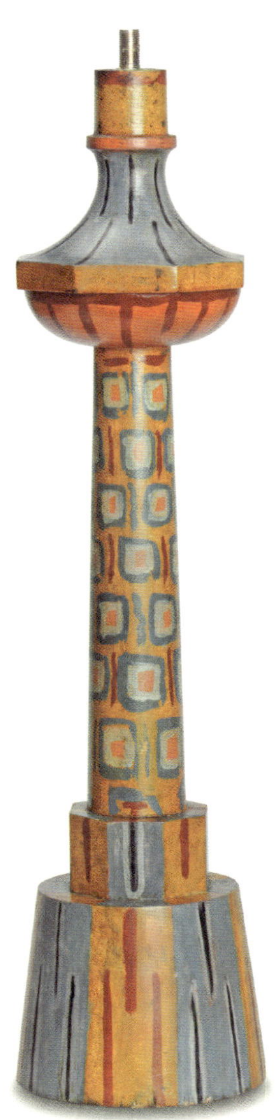

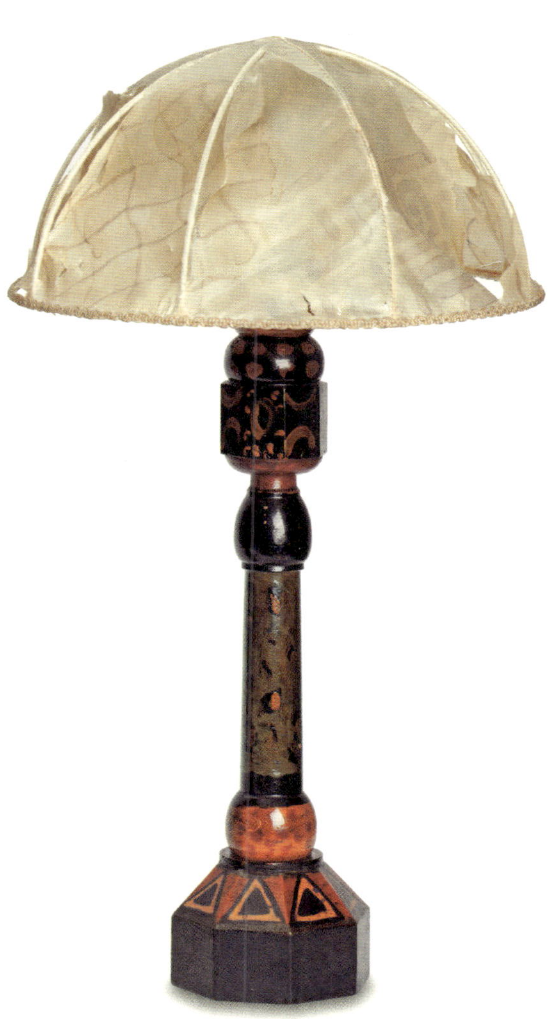

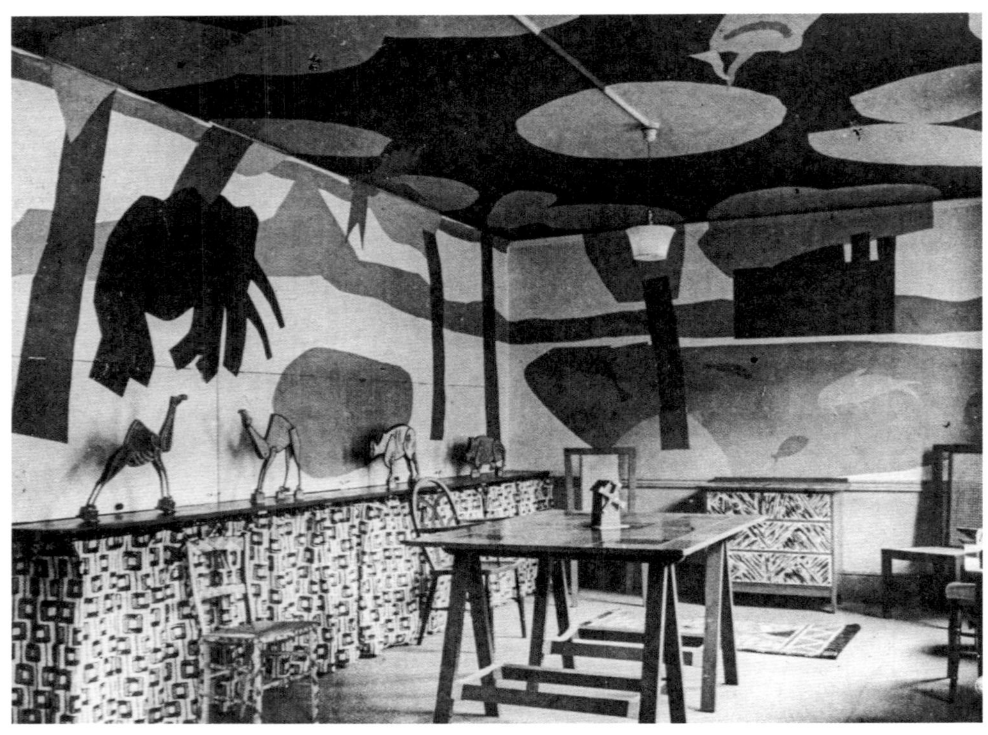

11. Model Nursery for Omega Workshops Ltd, 1913, walls and ceiling decorated by Vanessa Bell and Winifred Gill
Lantern slide
London Transport Museum
(2016/4376)

12. Roger Fry, design for a cabinet, 1913
Pencil, chalk, gouache and collage on tracing paper, 37.5 × 21.5 cm
Victoria and Albert Museum, London
(V&A: E.733-1955)
Given by Miss Margery Fry, J.P.

Bell and Winifred Gill decorated and furnished a nursery to underline that Omega style was suitable for all ages. Their jungle theme directly countered accusations that post-Impressionist art was childlike or 'primitive'. In her decoration of the walls and ceiling with brightly coloured paper shapes – anticipating the cut-outs made by French artist Henri Matisse – Bell was inspired by the way Omega designed marquetry and patterns (12). The nursery furniture seen in the surviving photograph was not specially designed for children, and even the toy camels and rhinoceroses seem ill-suited to play.

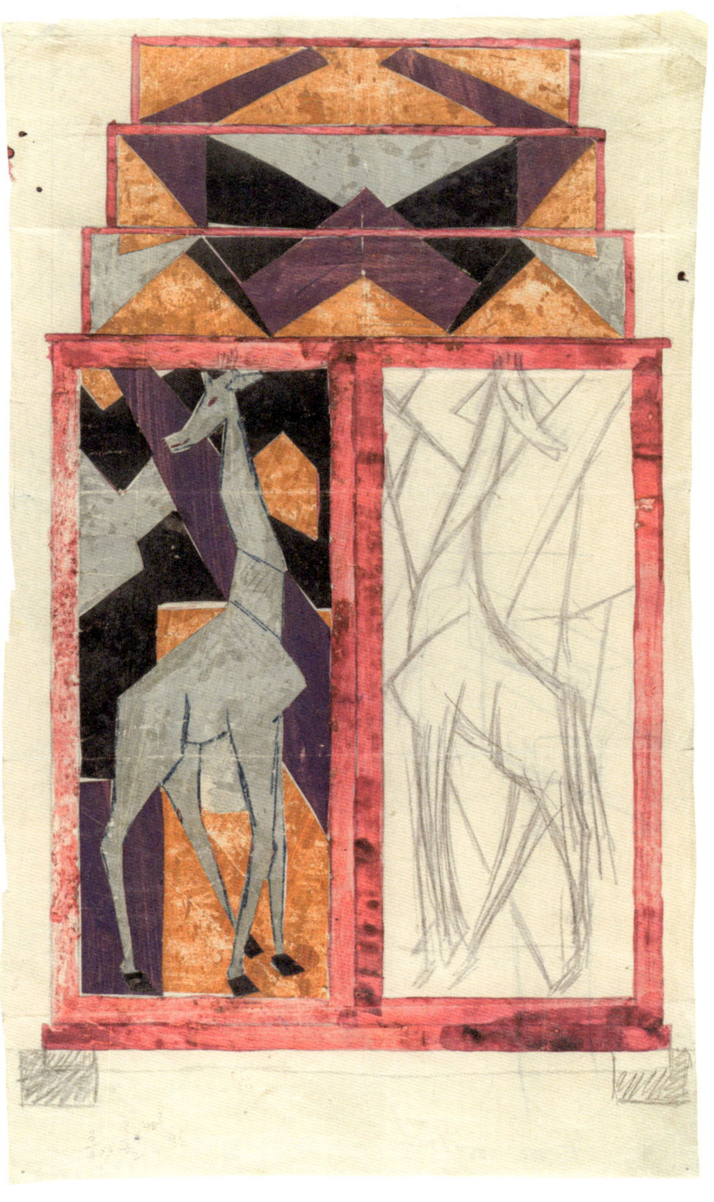

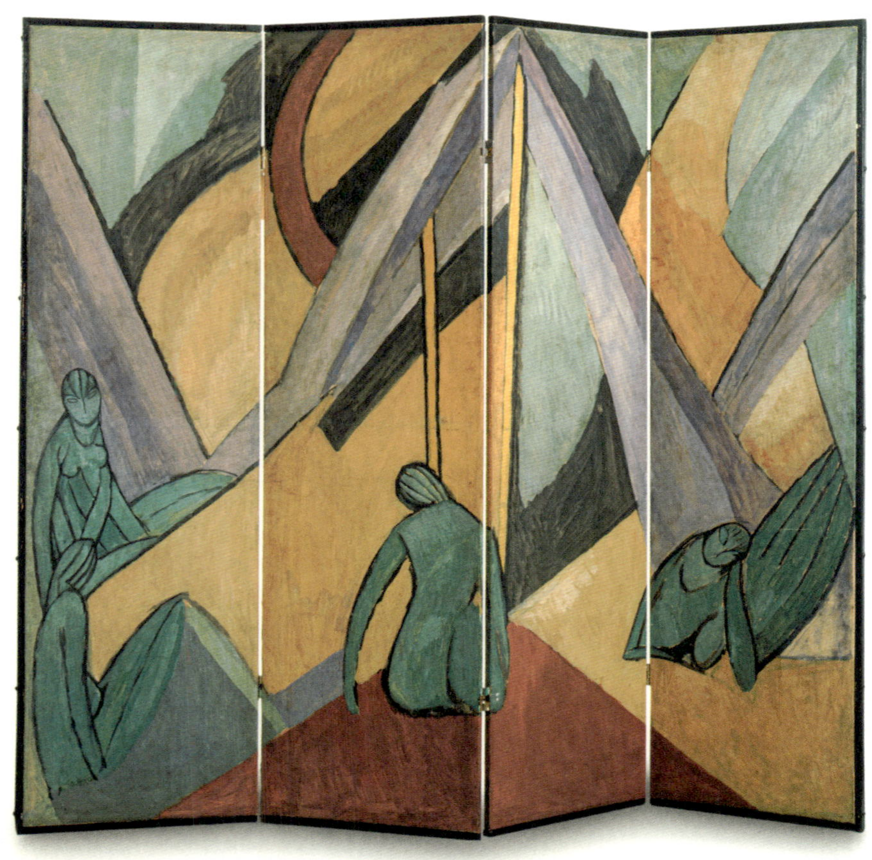

13. Screen, 1913, for Omega Workshops Ltd
Pencil and gouache on paper on canvas,
on four panels
Victoria and Albert Museum, London
(V&A: Circ.165-1964)

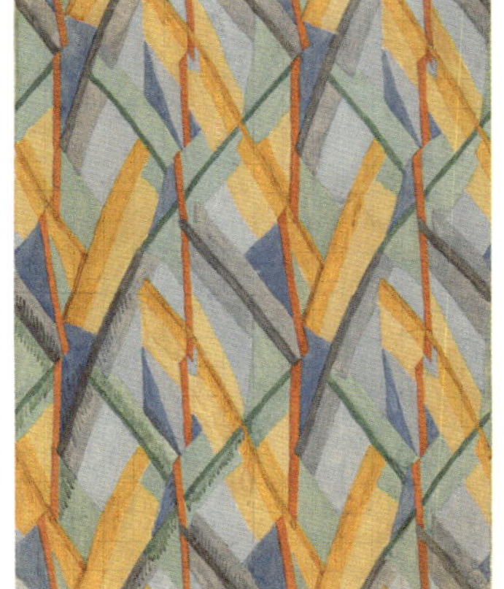

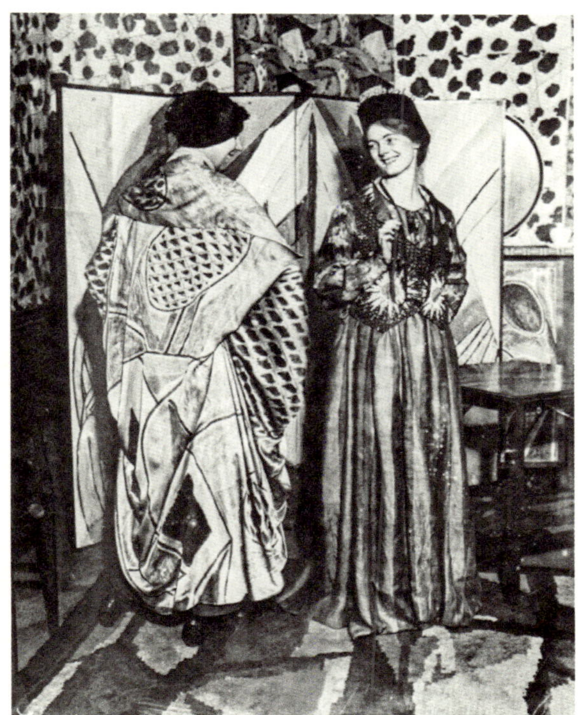

14. Design for a textile, 1913, for Omega Workshops Ltd
Watercolour, gouache and graphite on paper, 53.3 × 40.7 cm
Yale Center for British Art (B1992.14.2)

15. Nina Hamnett and Winifred Gill modelling Omega dresses at the Workshops in front of Bell's screen, illustrated in 'Women Who Do the Most Original Work', *Illustrated Sunday Herald* (October 1915)

Screens were prevalent at the Omega Workshops, offering artists a familiar scale and surface, and clients a flexible intervention in room arrangements (15). Bell's design, with its four green figures, has become known as an open-air bathing scene, a subject associated with Paul Cezanne and Henri Matisse. The original inspiration for this composition, as attested by the two central poles supporting a triangular structure, was a camping holiday in 1913. The flattened geometric forms of the tents arranged across the four panels were even further abstracted in a (probably unrealized) design for an Omega textile (14).

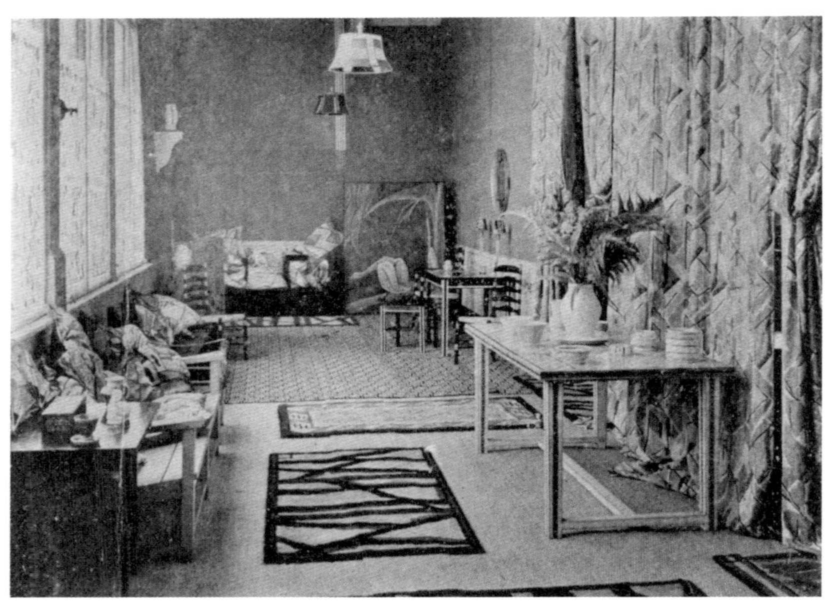

16. Holland Park Hall interior designed by Omega Workshops Ltd, 1914, in *Omega Workshops Ltd* (*c.* 1915) Victoria and Albert Museum, London (V&A NAL: 38041800109712)

17. Design for a carpet, 1914, for Omega Workshops Ltd
Gouache on paper, 44.8 × 24.5 cm
Victoria and Albert Museum, London
(V&A: E.725-1955)

18. Carpet, 1914, made by Wilton Royal Carpet Factory Ltd for Omega Workshops Ltd
Hooked woollen pile on jute warp and weft
Victoria and Albert Museum, London
(V&A: Circ.660-1962)

This entrance-hall rug (opposite) was part of an Omega decorative scheme commissioned by Lady Jean Hamilton (1861–1941) for her home at 1 Hyde Park Gardens, which included stained glass windows, floor mosaics and painted murals as well as furniture, lamps and textiles. For her carpet design, meticulously planned on graph paper, Bell continued the line of thought begun with the camping-inspired screen (13), allowing the outlines of the tents to become bold and black and thereby structuring the tripartite design. Multiples of this rug were produced so that one could also be displayed in the Allied Artists Association at Holland Park Hall (16).

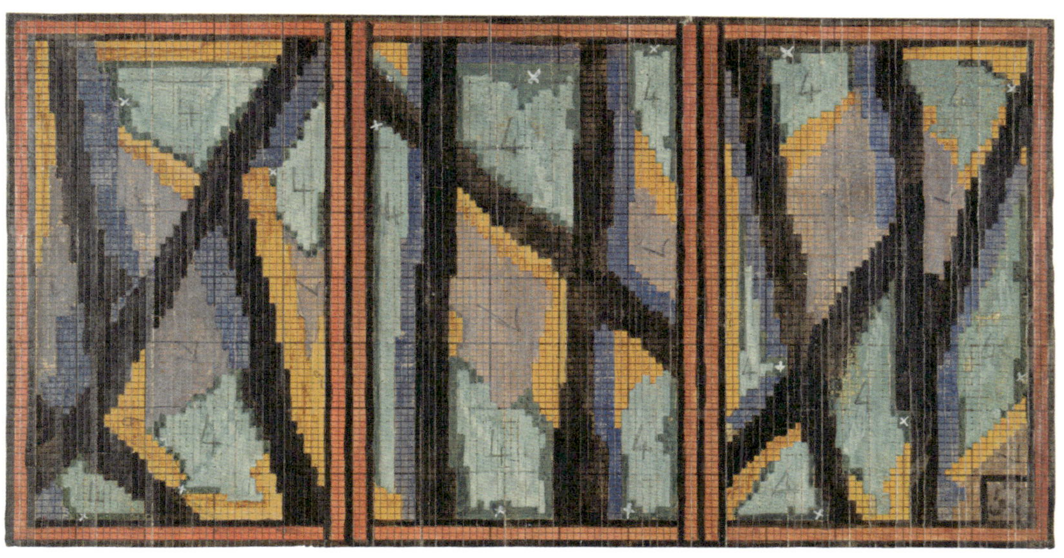

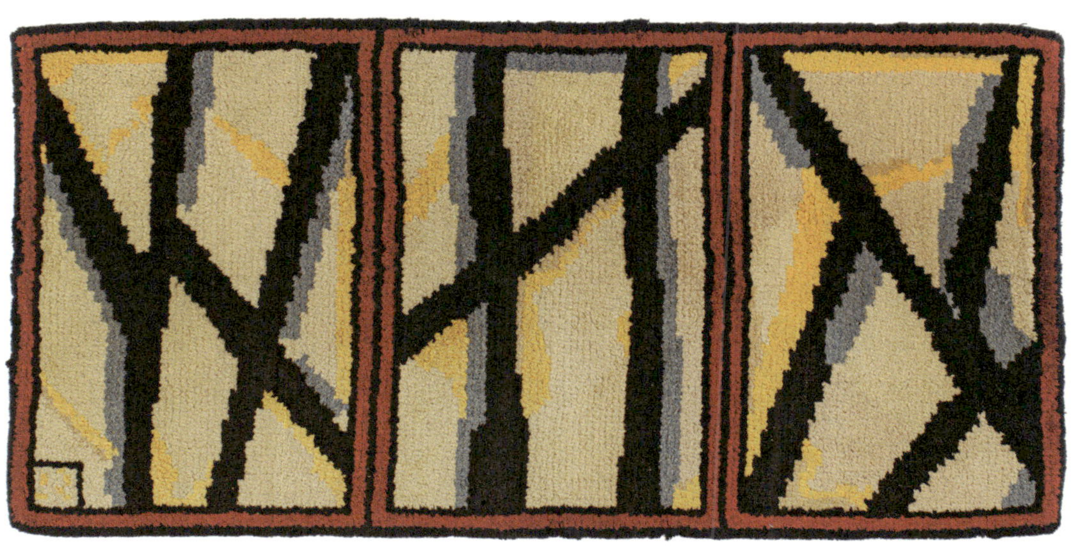

This fabric combines Bell's linear drawing and her instinctive use of colour in the laying of graphic geometrical forms over painterly splashes. Curtains of this fabric, in another colourway, featured in Omega's Ideal Home Exhibition display of 1913. In its cerise and green iteration, this fabric frames the French windows in a room that leads on to the Charleston garden, used by Bell as her bedroom in later life (46). The name 'white' was possibly in honour of the writer and suffragette Amber Blanco White, who rented a room at the top of the Omega building in Fitzroy Square.

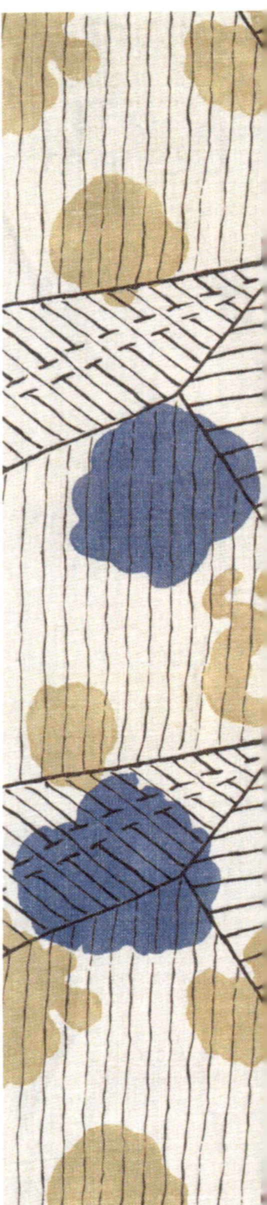

19. 'White' textile, 1913, made by Besselièvre for Omega Workshops Ltd
Printed linen
Victoria and Albert Museum, London
(V&A: T.84-1979)
Given by the Manchester Design Registry

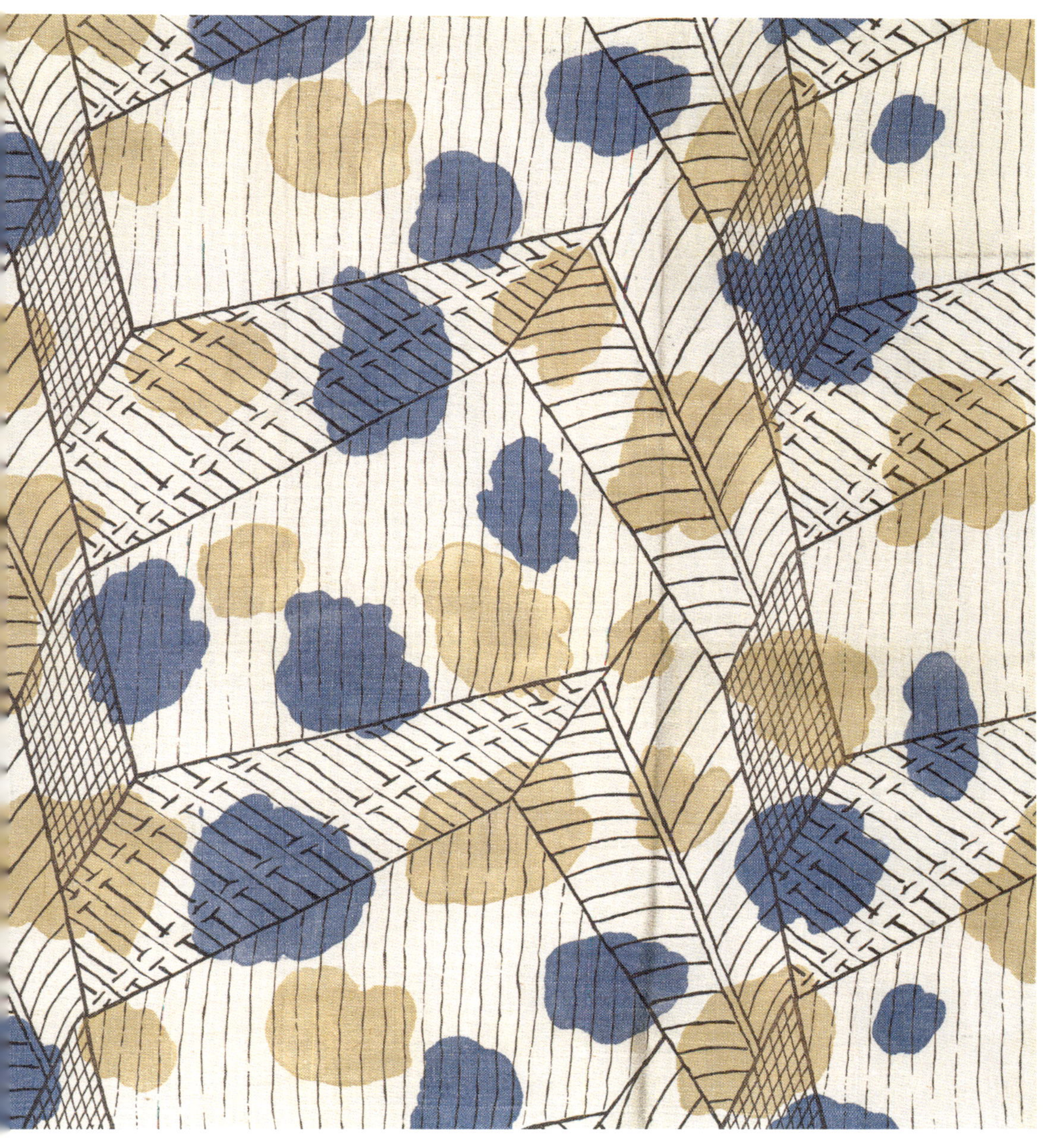

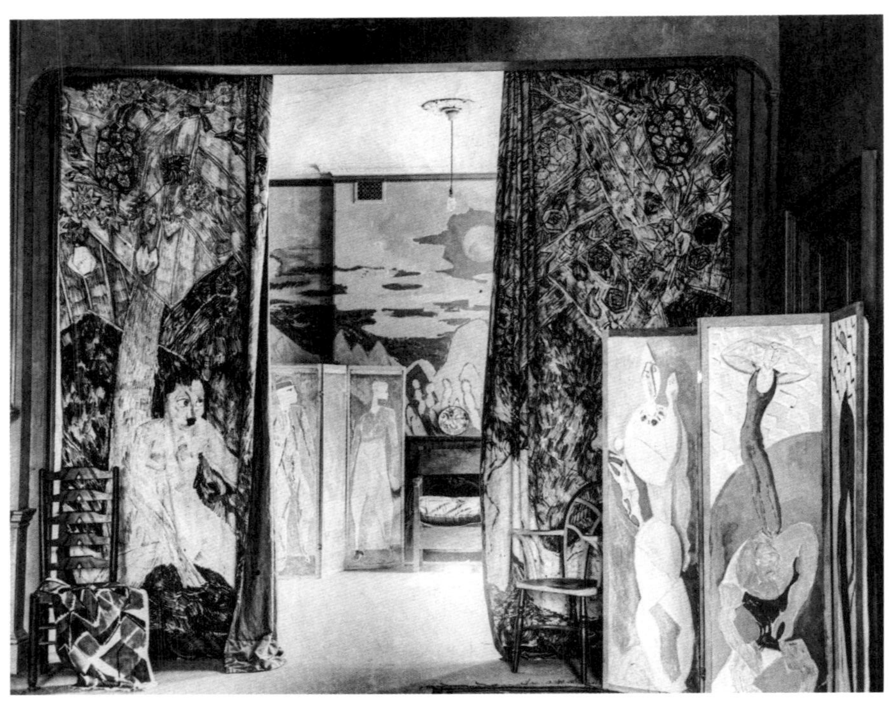

20. Opening room of the Omega Workshops, 33 Fitzroy Square, London, Charleston

21. 'Maud' textile, 1913, made by Besselièvre for Omega Workshops Ltd
Printed linen
Victoria and Albert Museum, London (V&A: Circ.425-1966)
Given by the Manchester Design Registry

The abstract geometrical forms of this fabric show Bell's interest in Cubism and collage. Printed in Rouen, it was produced in several high-keyed colourways, always with sharp black outlines. Bell and her circle showed the textile at the opening of the Omega Workshops (20), and used it to make cushions and curtains, as well as the pyjamas worn by Roger Fry to a party and costumes designed by Duncan Grant for Jacques Copeau's avant-garde production of *Twelfth Night* in Paris (1913). The fabric was very likely named after Omega customer Lady Maud Cunard, better known as Emerald, an American society hostess who lived in London.

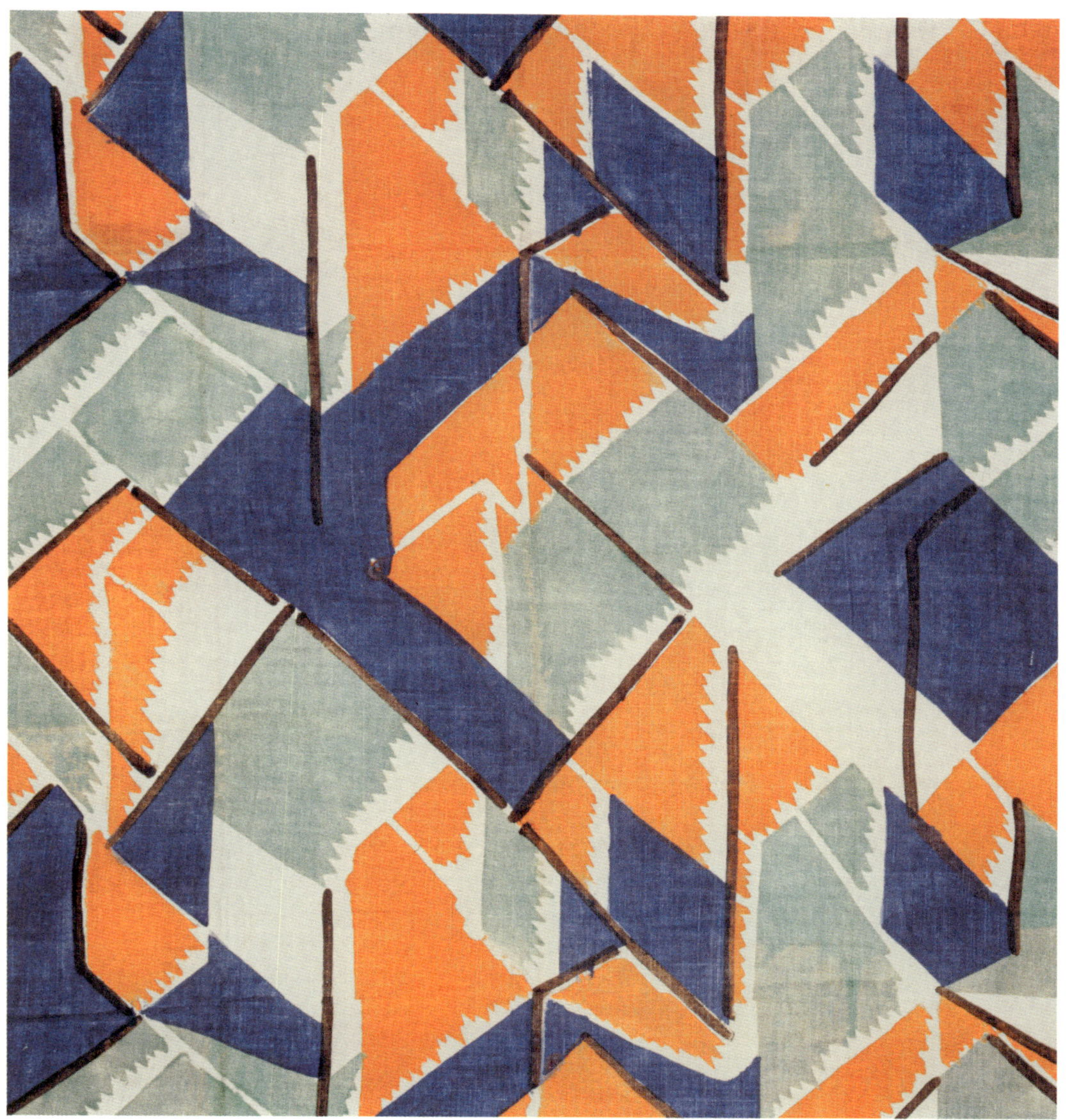

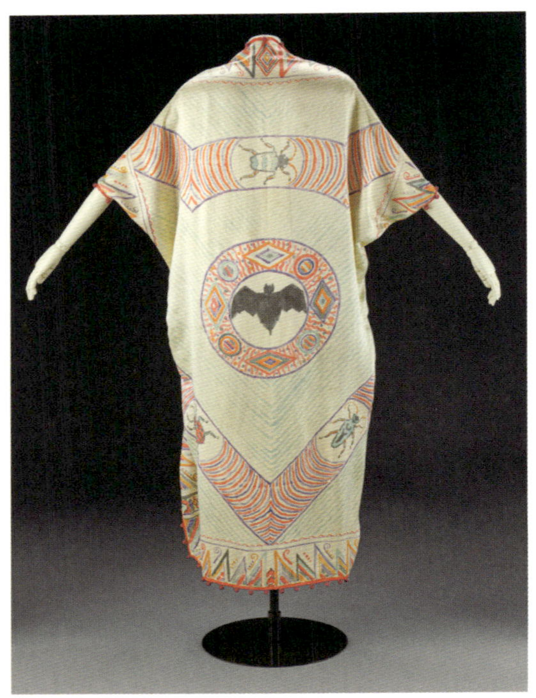

22. Robe, 1915–19, made by Omega Workshops Ltd
Hand-painted silk with wooden bead edging
Victoria and Albert Museum, London (V&A: T.118-2012)

From the Workshops' beginnings, Omega artists produced hand-painted and decorated clothing. Bell took on responsibility for Omega dress from 1915. Surviving garments are rare, although the boldness of their style can be seen in photographs (15) and is captured vividly in correspondence. In 1916 Woolf wrote to her sister 'My god! What clothes you are responsible for!'[29] This robe typifies the radically unstructured garments worn by fashionable European women in the 1910s. It features a bat and beetles, as well as the Ω itself, and the abstract patterns and bold colour palette typical of Omega.

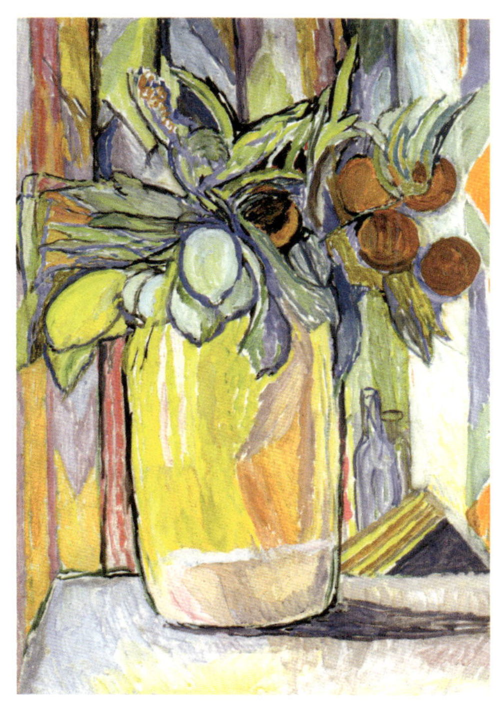

23. *Oranges and Lemons*, 1914
Oil on cardboard, 76 × 54 cm
Private collection

Bell often depicted fabrics and ceramics she collected on her travels alongside those she created herself. Here, an Italian vase sits in front of her 'Maud' fabric (21). In the pot are citrus fruits sent from Tunis by Grant, to whom she wrote: 'They are so lovely that against all modern theories I stuck them into my yellow Italian pot and at once began to paint them. I mean one isn't supposed nowadays to paint what one thinks beautiful.'[30] Despite these protestations, her modernism is evident in the picture's condensed space; the patterned backdrop is indistinguishable from some of the leaves and appears reflected in the ceramic glaze.

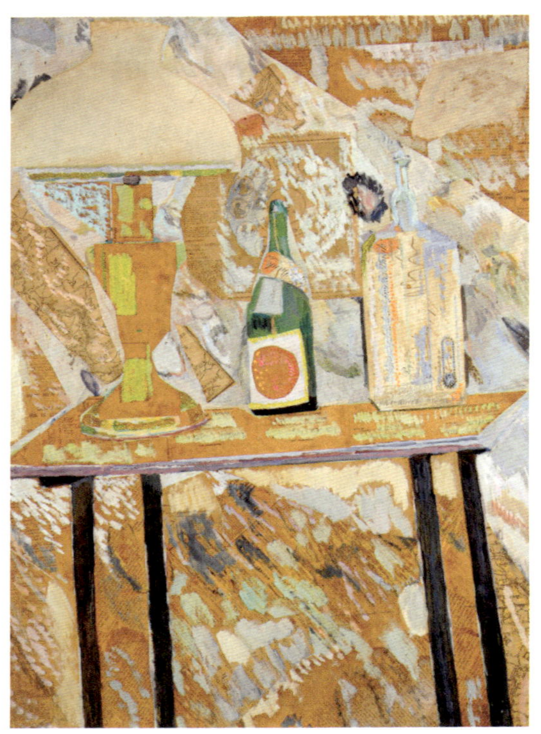

24. *Still Life (Triple Alliance)*, 1914
Collage, newsprint, oil and pastel on canvas, 81.9 × 60.3 cm
The University of Leeds Art Collection (LEEUA1923.1)

Bell sought to take modern art off the canvas and into daily life and rarely let things go the other way. She created this unusual still life of bottles from a collage of paper ephemera. Some fragments are personal – a cheque made out to herself for five guineas – while others reflect current events. Bell made this work in late summer 1914, when Britain was on the brink of the First World War, as is evident in the newspaper cutting from *The Times* for 1 September and maps of the Meuse Valley in France. The title, *Triple Alliance*, references the entente signed by Britain, France and Russia.

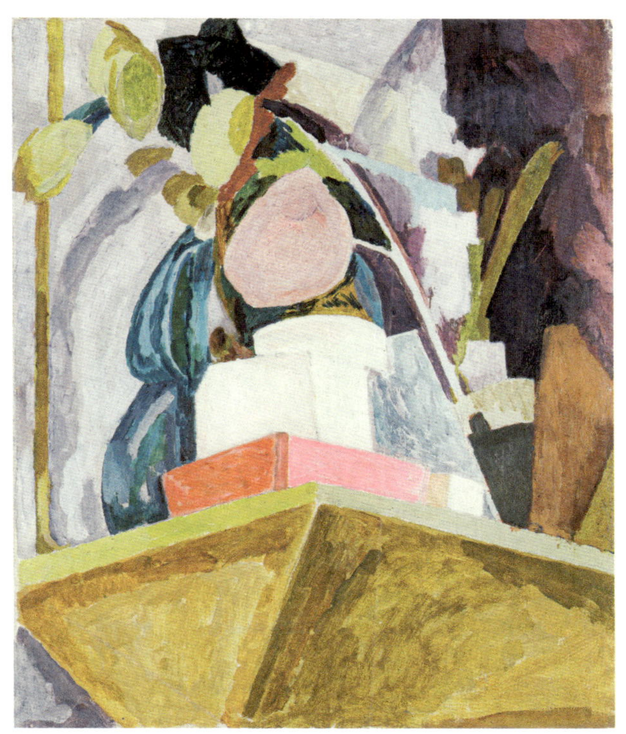

25. Still Life on Corner of a Mantelpiece, 1914
Oil on canvas, 55.9 × 45.7 cm
Tate
(T01133)

Looking up at the mantelpiece in her studio at Gordon Square, Bell turned a conglomeration of domestic items, boxes, cartons and flowers in a vase into a monumental, if almost abstract, pyramid arrangement. Each form is simplified, with the scrolled moulding under the shelf distilled into two trapezoids. The bloom at centre seems to have no petals, and was in fact one of the decorative fake flowers produced by Bell and other members of the Omega Workshops. Bell painted this still life alongside her friend Grant, whose rendering is less abstract.

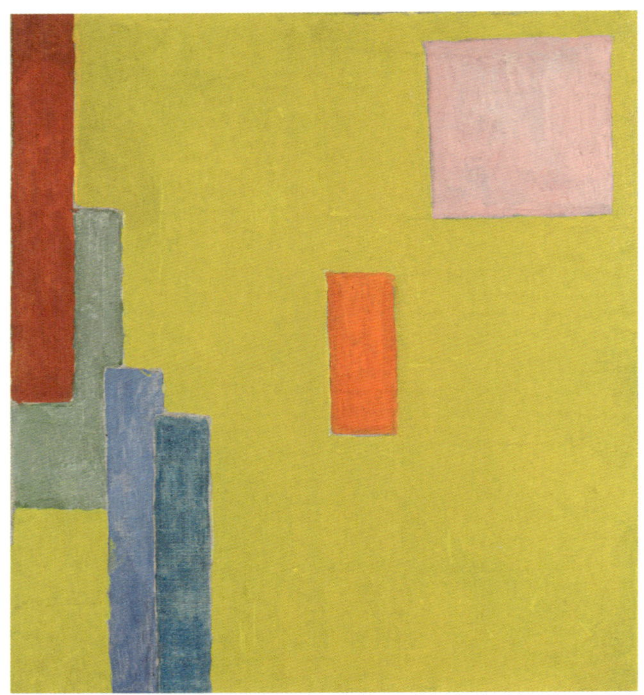

26. *Abstract Painting*, *c.* 1914
Oil on canvas, 44.1 × 38.7 cm
Tate
(T01935)

While working on Omega designs, Bell continued to paint, admitting to Fry, 'It's rather fun painting after doing all these patterns.'[31] Creating abstract textiles led her to experiment with non-figurative painting. The warm- and cool-toned rectangles of this work sit comfortably on their yellow background yet, as in the Omega textiles, the colours are far from flat, and the canvas weave is prominent. In 1914 Bell's husband Clive published a book simply called *Art*, in which he outlined the importance of 'significant form', meaning 'lines and colours combined in a particular way, certain forms and relations of forms, [that] stir our aesthetic emotions'.[32]

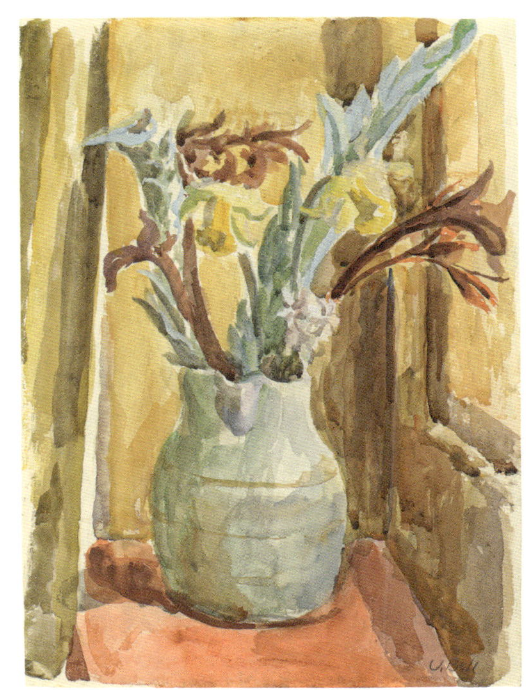

27. *Flower Piece*, *c.* 1915–30
Watercolour on paper, 35.3 × 25.4 cm
Victoria and Albert Museum, London
(V&A: P.45-1931)
From the collection of the late Captain
Desmond Coke

This simple arrangement of daffodils and gladioli in a white jug on a red window sill probably dates from a later period than the more compositionally complex *Still Life with Wild Flowers* (**29**). Working in watercolour, Bell has again used the white of the paper as part of her composition. In one of her rare lectures on art, Bell used drawing a flower as an example of the limits of mechanical reproduction: 'If you are capable of seeing that flower with all its subtleties of form, the way its edges recede or are sharp against the space behind, you have to try to express your feeling about those things in line.'[33]

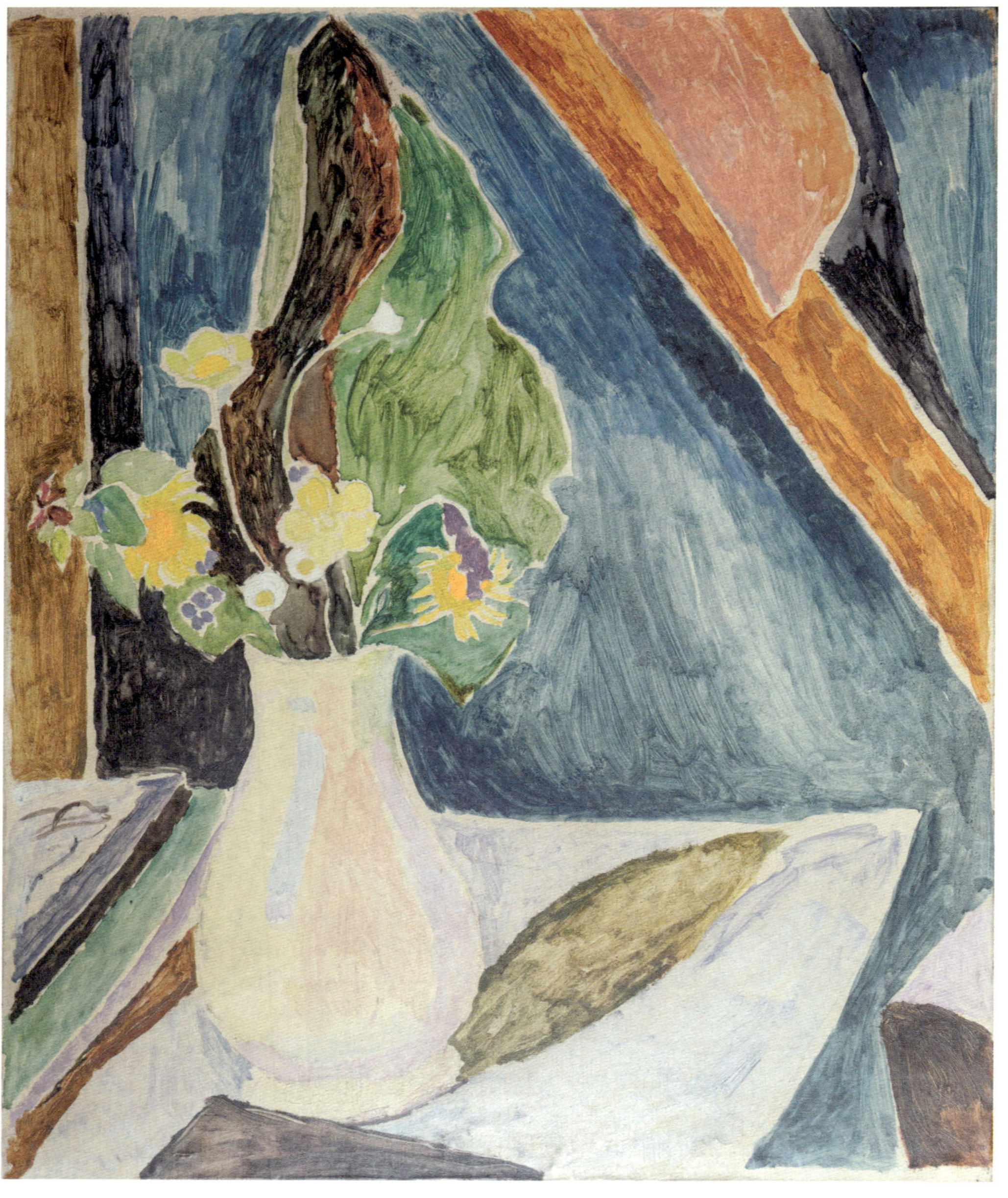

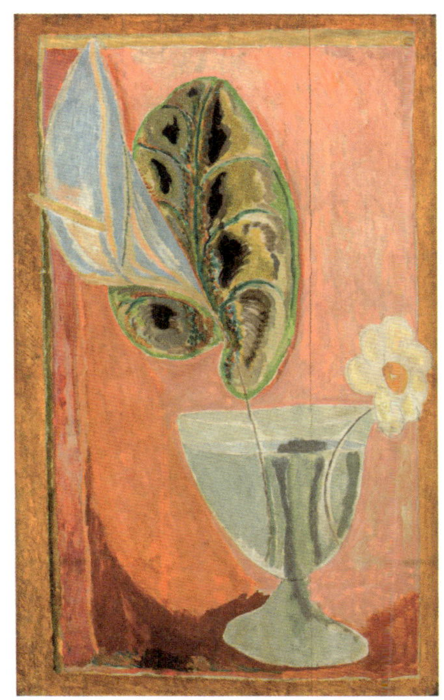

28. *Still Life with Wild Flowers*, 1915
Oil on canvas, 76.2 × 63.5 cm
Charleston
(CHA/P/1241)

29. Duncan Grant, Omega Workshops Ltd sign, 1913
Oil on wood, 108.5 × 67.2 cm
Victoria and Albert Museum, London
(V&A: P.35-1963)

Bell very likely painted these delicate wild flowers while staying in the Sussex countryside home of Mary Hutchinson. The composition makes a feature of the room's perpendicular and diagonal beams, which echo the forms of the large leaves framing the smaller flowers. Bell experimented with leaving bare canvas to delineate forms, and using loose brushwork, varying the opacity of paint over the blue wall. Two years previously, Grant had painted a similarly loose floral arrangement on the reverse of the Omega signboard (above). Bell's *Wild Flowers* would later hang on his bedroom wall at Charleston, where it remains today.

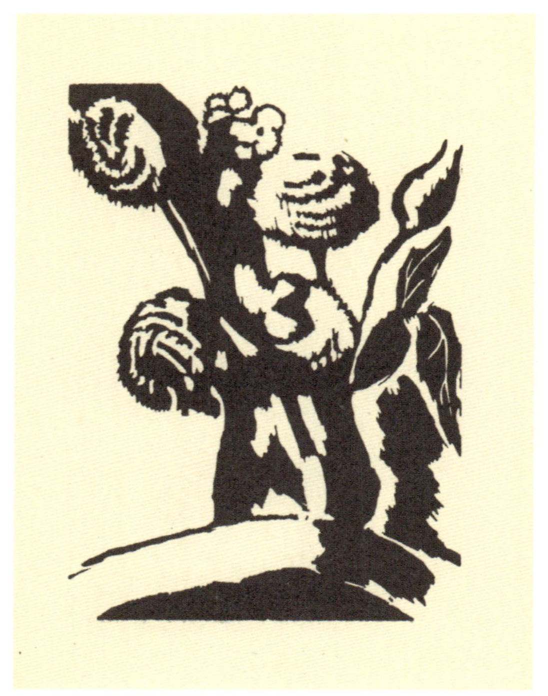

30. *Dahlias*, 1918, for Omega Workshops Ltd
Woodcut on paper, 26 × 18.7 cm
Victoria and Albert Museum, London
(V&A: E.2624-1962)

Dahlias and *Nude* (31) appeared in the Omega publication *Original Woodcuts by Various Artists* in 1918 alongside the work of Fry, Grant and others. This was the fourth book Fry had published featuring woodcuts; since the Arts and Crafts movement this technique of using hand-carved printing blocks had attracted modern artists, especially in Britain, who preferred its eccentricities to photomechanical reproductions. *Dahlias* further simplifies the composition of Bell's painting *Still Life on Corner of a Mantelpiece* (25) into stark monochrome. Bell's letters to Fry suggest she was self-conscious about the quality of her woodcuts, which he highly esteemed.[34]

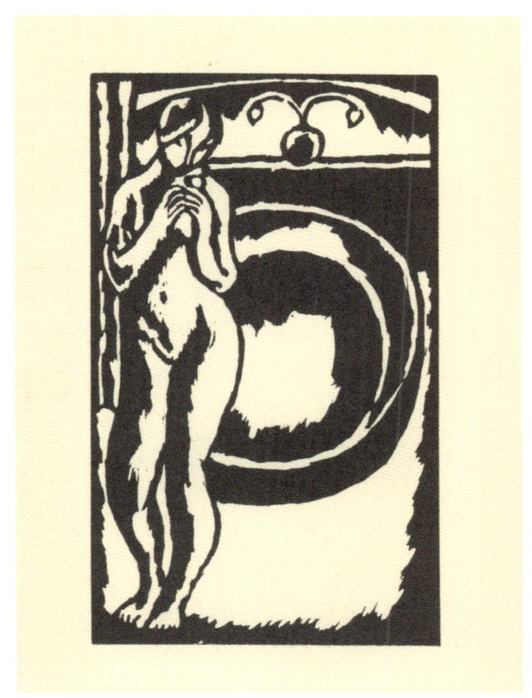

31. *Nude*, 1918, for Omega Workshops Ltd
Woodcut on paper, 26 × 18.7 cm
Victoria and Albert Museum, London
(V&A: E.2631-1962)

Bell was seemingly encouraged in making woodcuts by her Omega colleague Winifred Gill. In a letter to Gill in November 1918, she wrote, 'I am looking forward to trying to do some more wood cutting, for London is too hopelessly dark in the winter that one can't paint half the time.'[35] In her woodcuts, Bell played with compositions she had already tried out on canvas. In *Nude*, she compresses the configuration of woman and tub found in *The Tub* (33), simplifying the still life in the background from three flowers to two.

This mural-sized painting was originally planned as a decoration for the Garden Room at Charleston, but Bell never installed her 'big bath picture'. Bell's painting shows concern for the careful arrangement of forms: the room is composed of abstract shapes, the tub on the floor is viewed from above so that it becomes almost circular, and she has painted out incidental details such as the woman's chemise and a jug once between the tub and the woman. The pose of the model, Mary Hutchinson, is taken from Matisse's *Le Luxe II*, painted a decade before and shown at the *Second Post-Impressionist Exhibition* in 1912 (below).

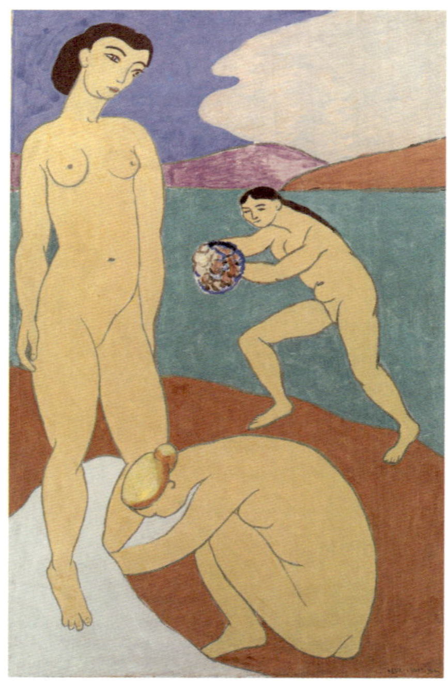

32. Henri Matisse, *Le Luxe II*, 1907–8
Distemper on canvas, 209.5 × 139 cm
Statens Museum for Kunst, Copenhagen
(KMSr76)

33. *The Tub*, 1917
Oil on canvas, 180.3 × 166.4 cm
Tate
(T02010)

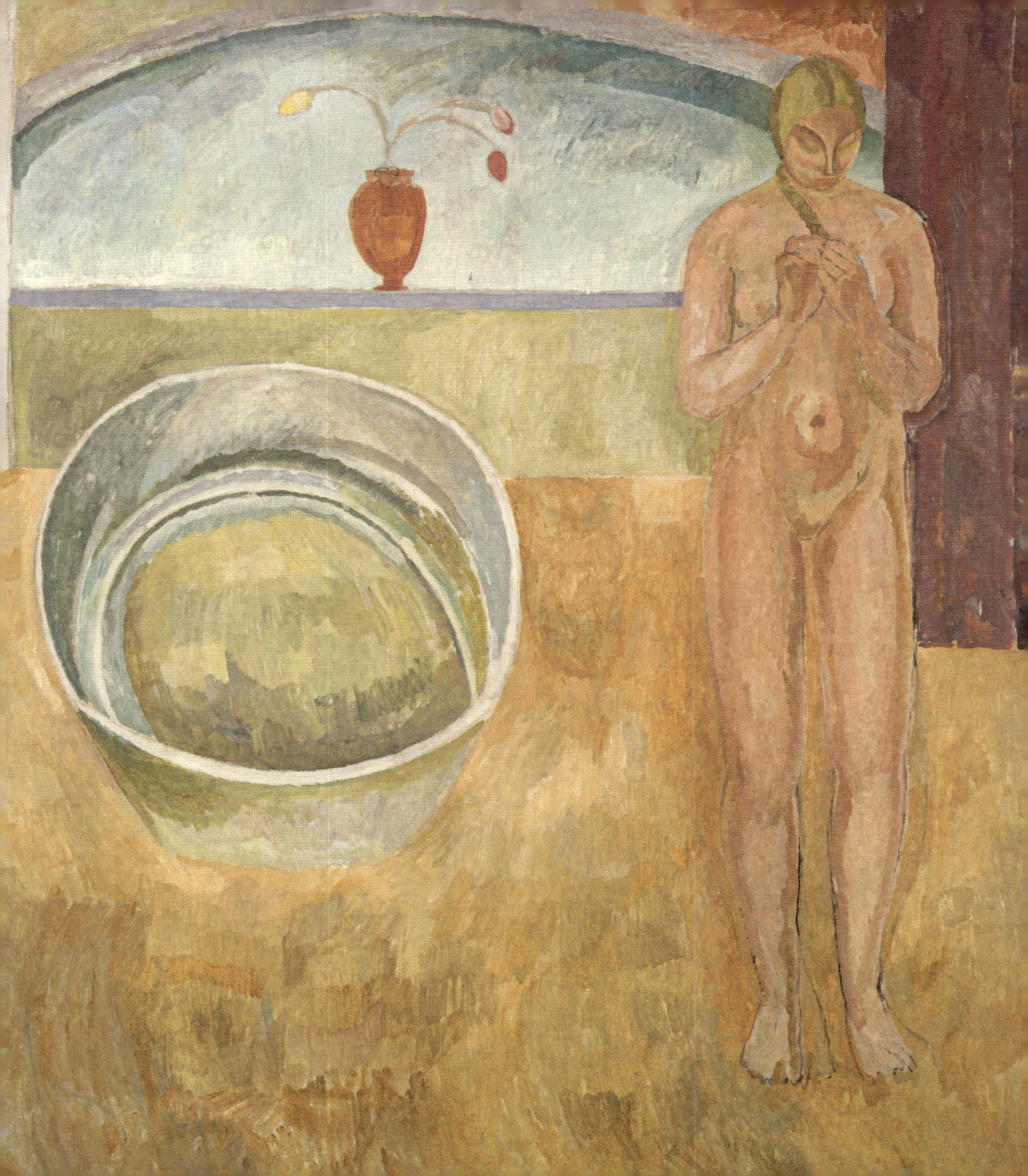

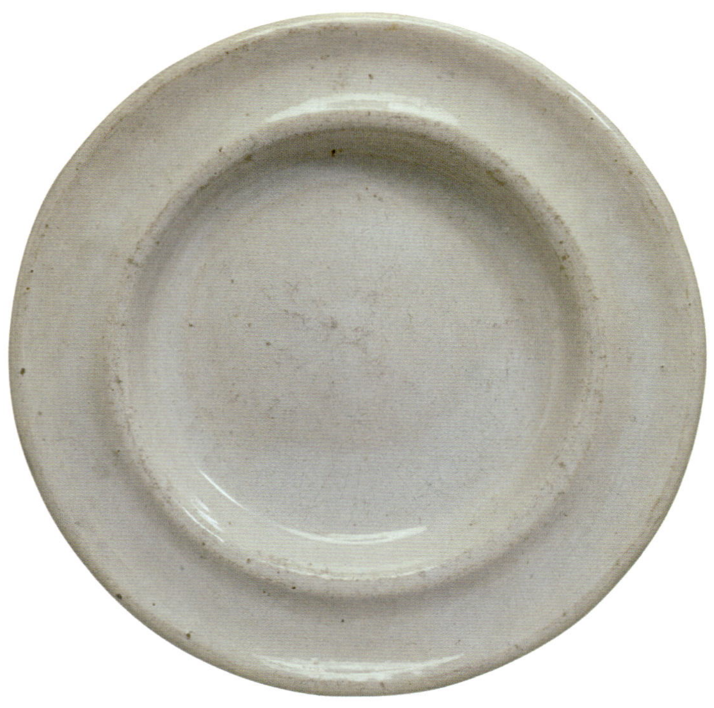

34. Plate, *c.* 1914–15, probably thrown by Roger Fry for the Omega Workshops
Tin-glazed earthenware
Victoria and Albert Museum, London
(V&A: Circ.250-1958)
Given by Pamela Diamand, daughter of Roger Fry

35. *Study of a Woman*, c. 1917
Oil on canvas, 29.4 × 23 cm
Charleston
(CHA/P/5233)

The circular forms that dominate the left-hand side of this portrait are plates. Simple and broad-rimmed in shape, and grey-white in glazing, they resemble those made for the Omega Workshops probably by Roger Fry (34). Vanessa Bell owned a set (which she used at Charleston and displayed in the dresser there), as did her friend Mary Hutchinson, who sat for numerous portraits by Bell in this period, once owned this painting and may in fact be the model. The presence of the plates emphasizes that they connected members of Bell's circle both aesthetically and socially.

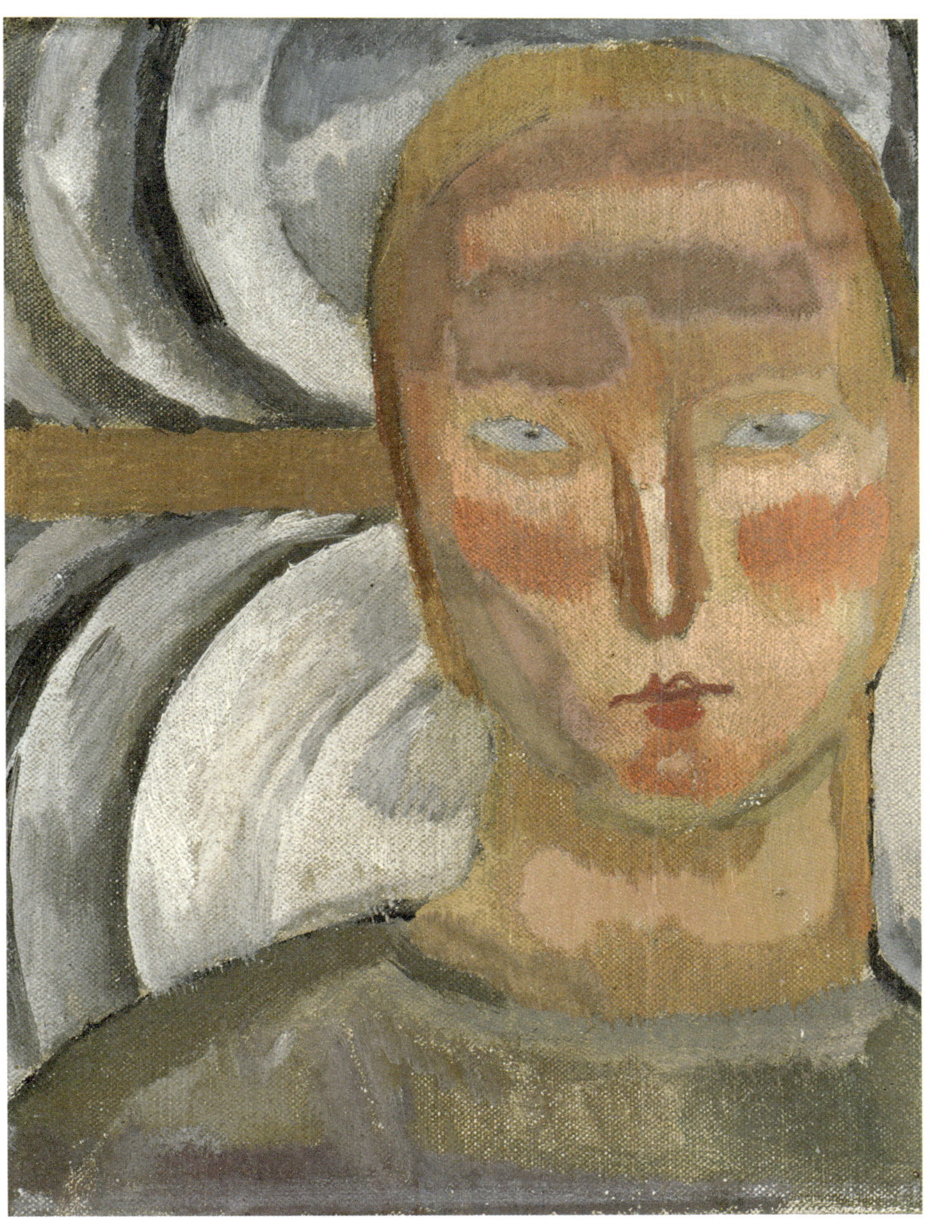

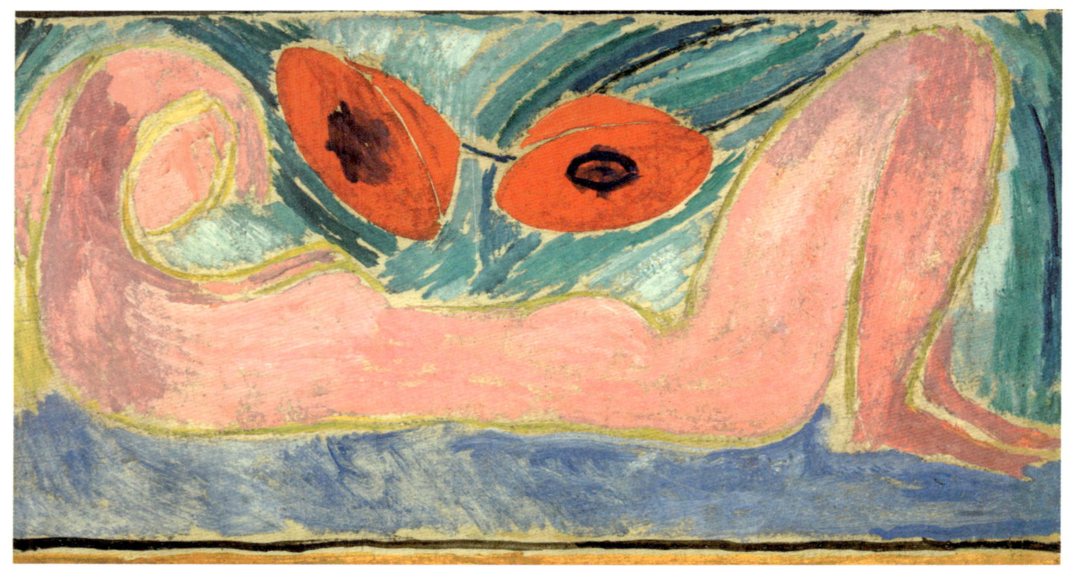

36. *Nude with Poppies*, 1916
Oil on canvas, 23.5 × 42.5 cm
Swindon Museum and Art Gallery
(AG1973/294)

37. Bed, probably designed by Roger Fry for Omega Workshops Ltd, 1915–16
Oil on wood, cast iron
Victoria and Albert Museum, London
(V&A: Circ.270 to F-1975)
Bequeathed by Mrs F. C. O. Speyer

This study for a single bedhead was part of a wider suite of decorations Bell undertook with Grant for St John and Mary Hutchinson between 1916 and 1919, while Mary was having an affair with Clive Bell. The Hutchinson home, River House, was in Hammersmith, an area with an Arts and Crafts legacy. Perhaps for this reason, Bell saw in this bedhead echoes of Frederic Lord Leighton's eminently Victorian painting *Flaming June* (1895), despite the evidently post-Impressionist stylization of forms and loose brushwork. Bedsteads were popular with Omega painters and Bell was not alone in exploiting their sensuous associations (37).

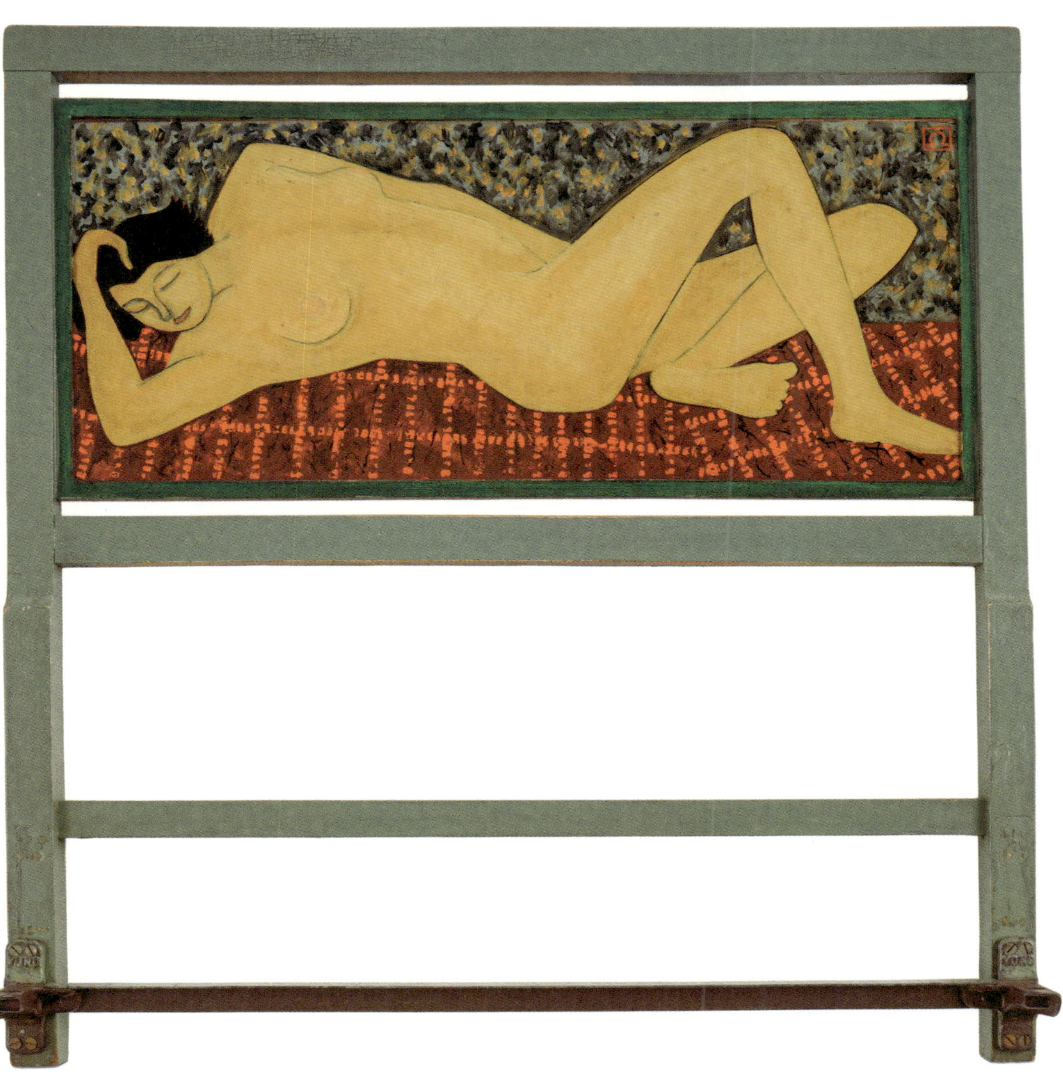

According to Duncan Grant, this was the first work Bell painted after they moved to Charleston in October 1916. When describing their new home to Grant in the weeks prior, she began by noting 'a large lake', adding 'The colour is too amazing now, all very warm, most lovely browns and warm greys and red with the chalk everywhere giving that odd kind of softness.'[36] This palette and the abstracting effects of the reflecting waters are readily apparent in this picture, which also features the dark triangle of the granary roof and ochre oblong of a ridge of the South Downs in the background.

38. *The Pond, Charleston*, 1916
Oil on canvas, 29.5 × 34.8 cm
Charleston
(CHA/P/78)

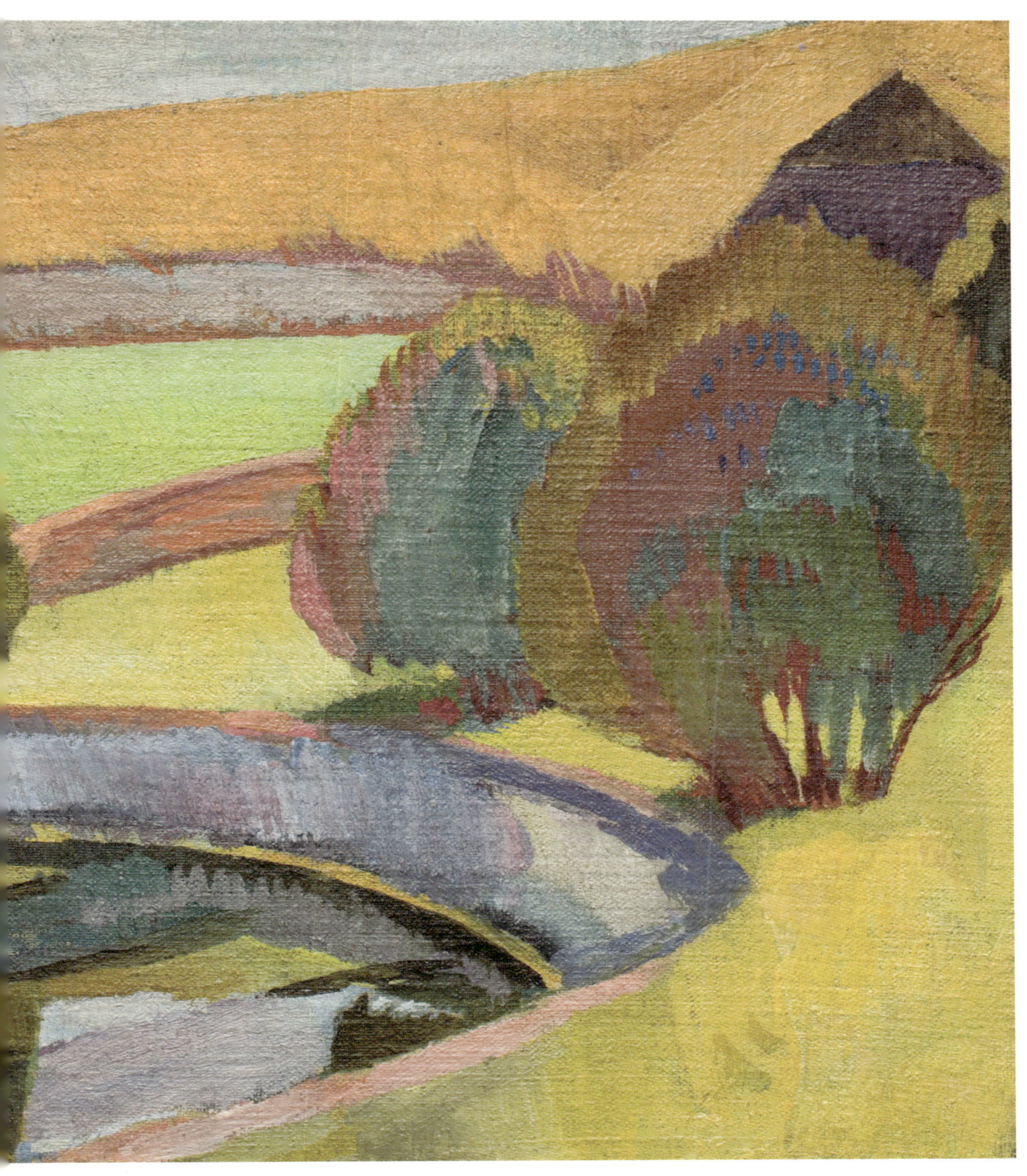

Bell has composed this watercolour carefully, so that the pond itself appears as a horizontal strip across the bottom third of the paper, reflecting the almost symmetrical trees above. This most likely shows the pond at Charleston, a subject of ongoing fascination for Bell. Despite the sparseness of this image, her touches of watercolour are in a high-keyed palette. They are not closely tethered to the forms they depict and border on abstraction, demonstrating how carefully Bell studied Paul Cezanne's use of watercolour (39).

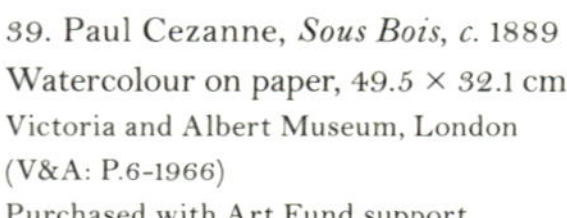

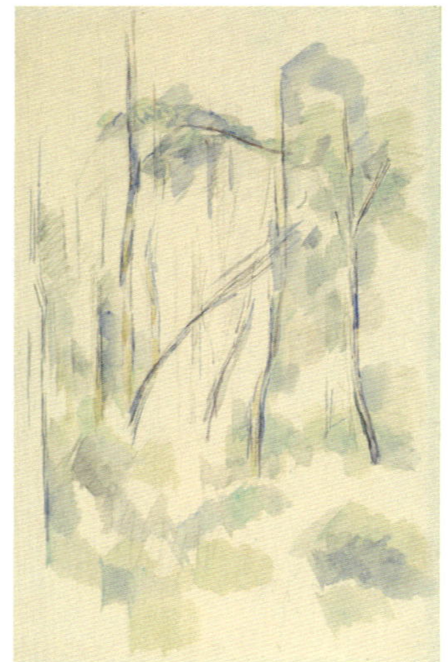

39. Paul Cezanne, *Sous Bois*, *c.* 1889
Watercolour on paper, 49.5 × 32.1 cm
Victoria and Albert Museum, London
(V&A: P.6-1966)
Purchased with Art Fund support

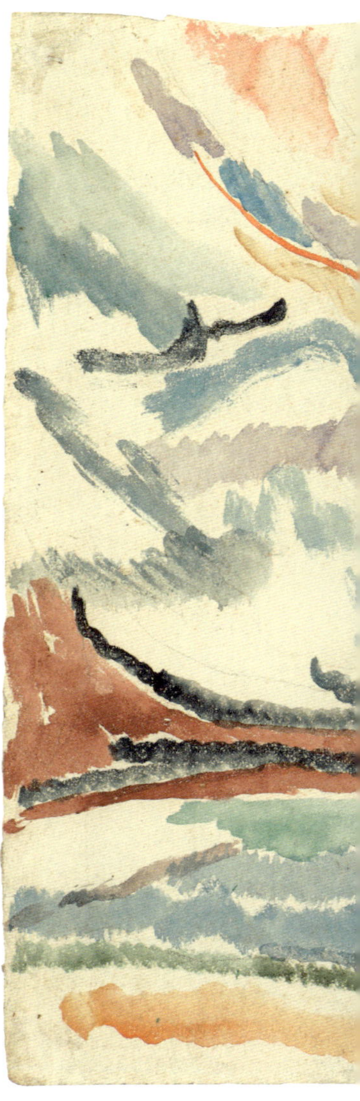

40. *Landscape, Trees by a Pond*, 1916
Watercolour on paper, 38.3 × 55.4 cm
Victoria and Albert Museum, London
(V&A: Circ.519-1963)

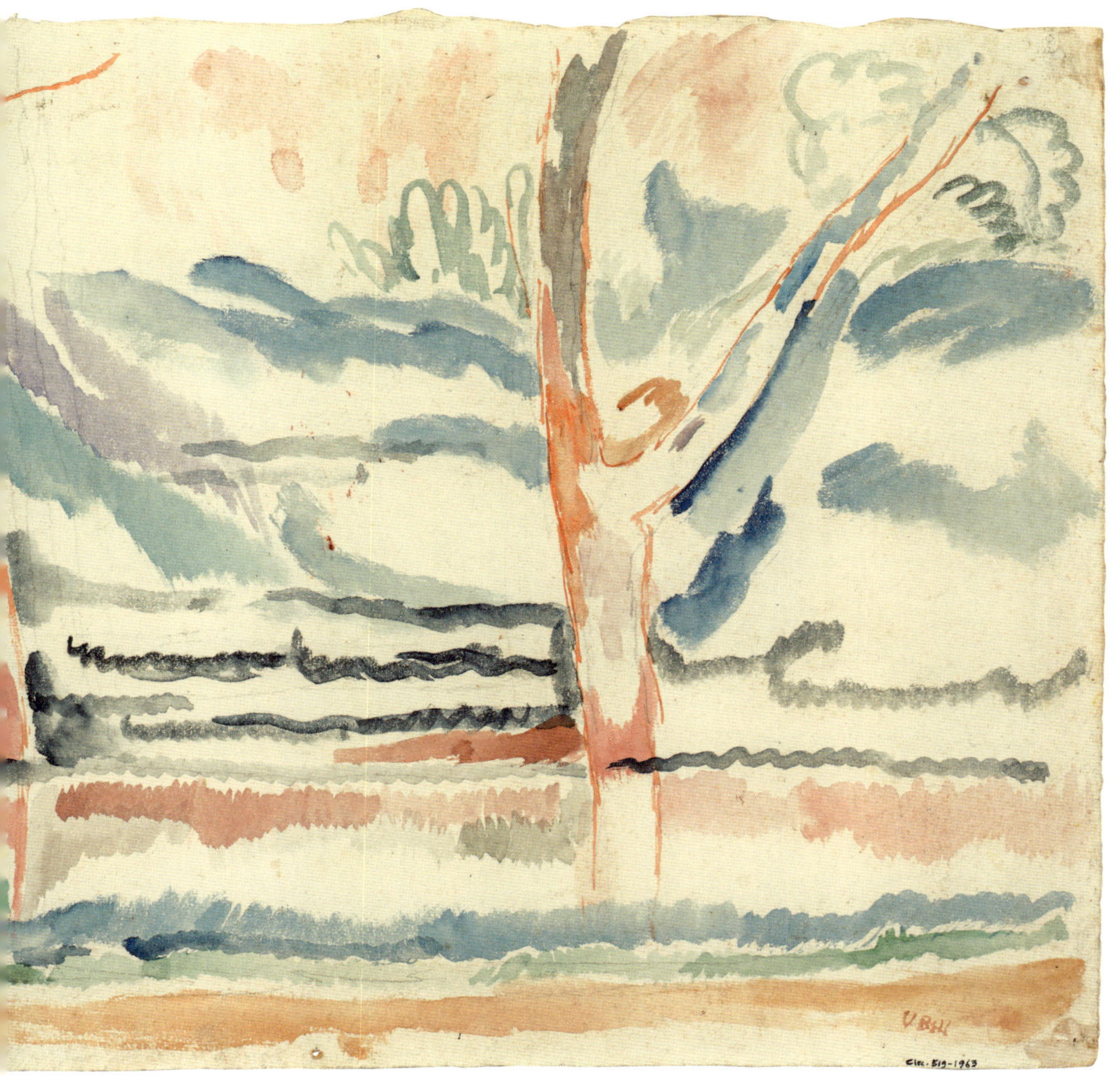
V Bell
Circ. 519-1963

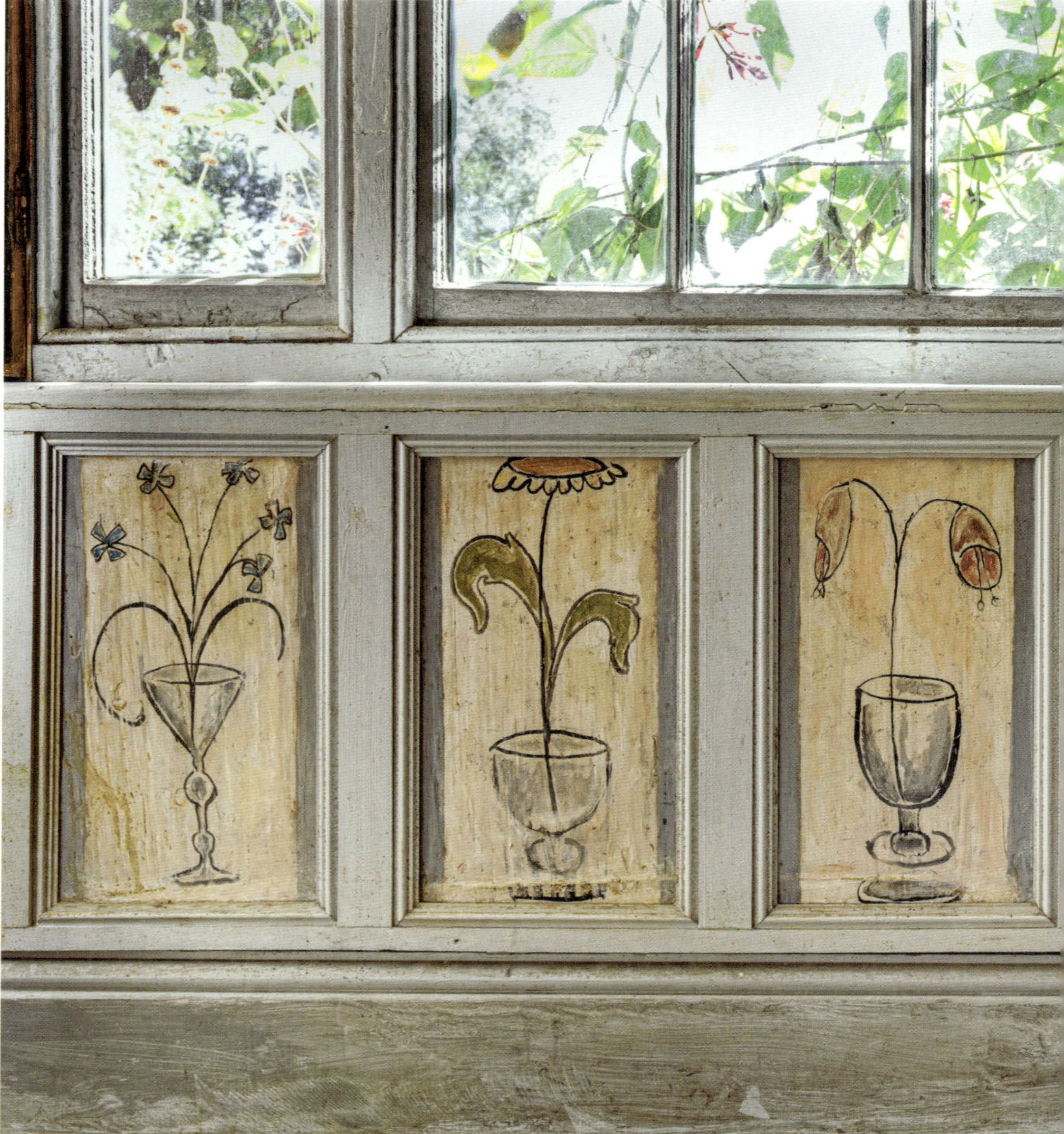

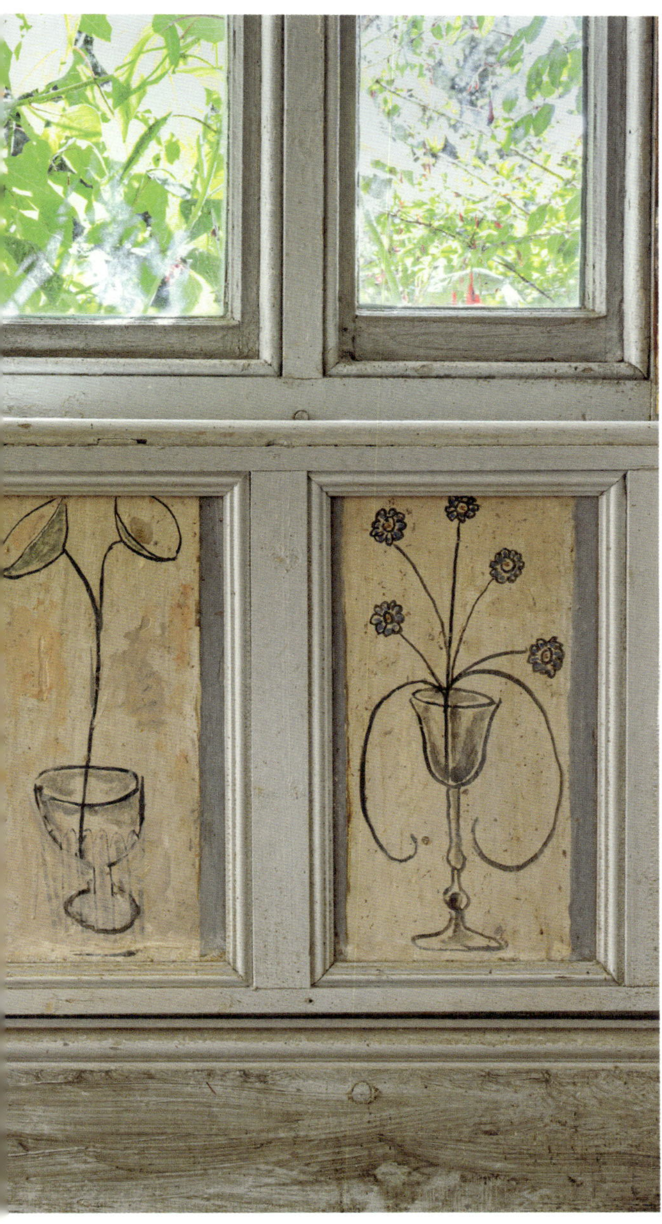

These decorations were some of the first Bell undertook at Charleston. They brightened up the ground-floor room used for teaching her children, which later became Clive Bell's study. Below the window, each panel features a single stylized bloom with a slim stem standing improbably tall in a wine glass. Through the surface of the paint, a previous idea to depict fluted glasses is still visible. The window embrasure is painted in abstract geometrical forms in dusty pink, mustard yellow and periwinkle blue, and striped shades of pink, purple, blue and grey appear along the lintel.

41. Window decorations, 1916–17, Charleston
(CHA/DEC/2c1-7)

The key to the harmony of this design for Duncan Grant's bedroom is found in the colour scheme. The walls are not white but grey, a colour Bell and Grant achieved by mixing Indian red and cobalt blue into white paint. This subtle mid-tone – similar to the colour of Cezanne's studio in Aix-en-Provence – both absorbs and reflects light, and ensures the freshness of surrounding colours. Bell used the same colour as the ground for her freely painted floral arrangements and marbled circles on the two doors. The Indian red skirting boards and door frames bring the scheme together. Above the fireplace hangs a copy of Raphael's *St Catherine of Alexandria* (*c.* 1507) in the National Gallery, London, painted by Bell around 1922.

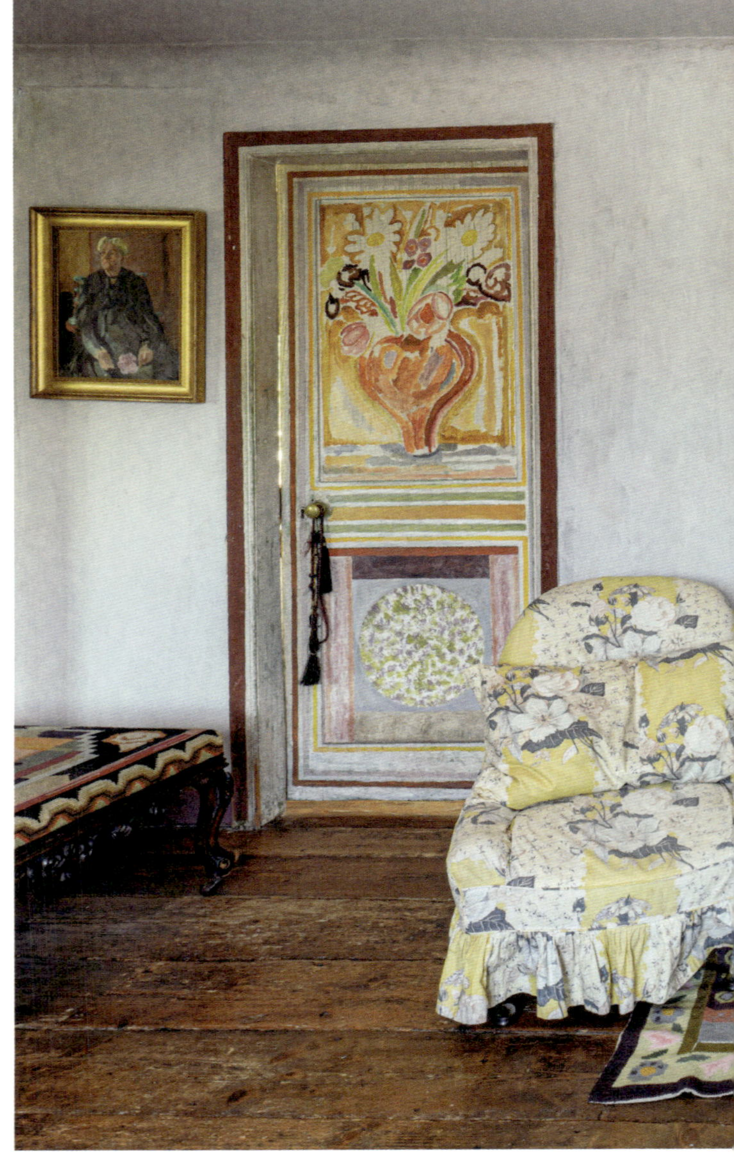

42. Fireplace (1918) and door (1920–25) decorations, Charleston (CHA/F/139; CHA/DEC/14a-b)

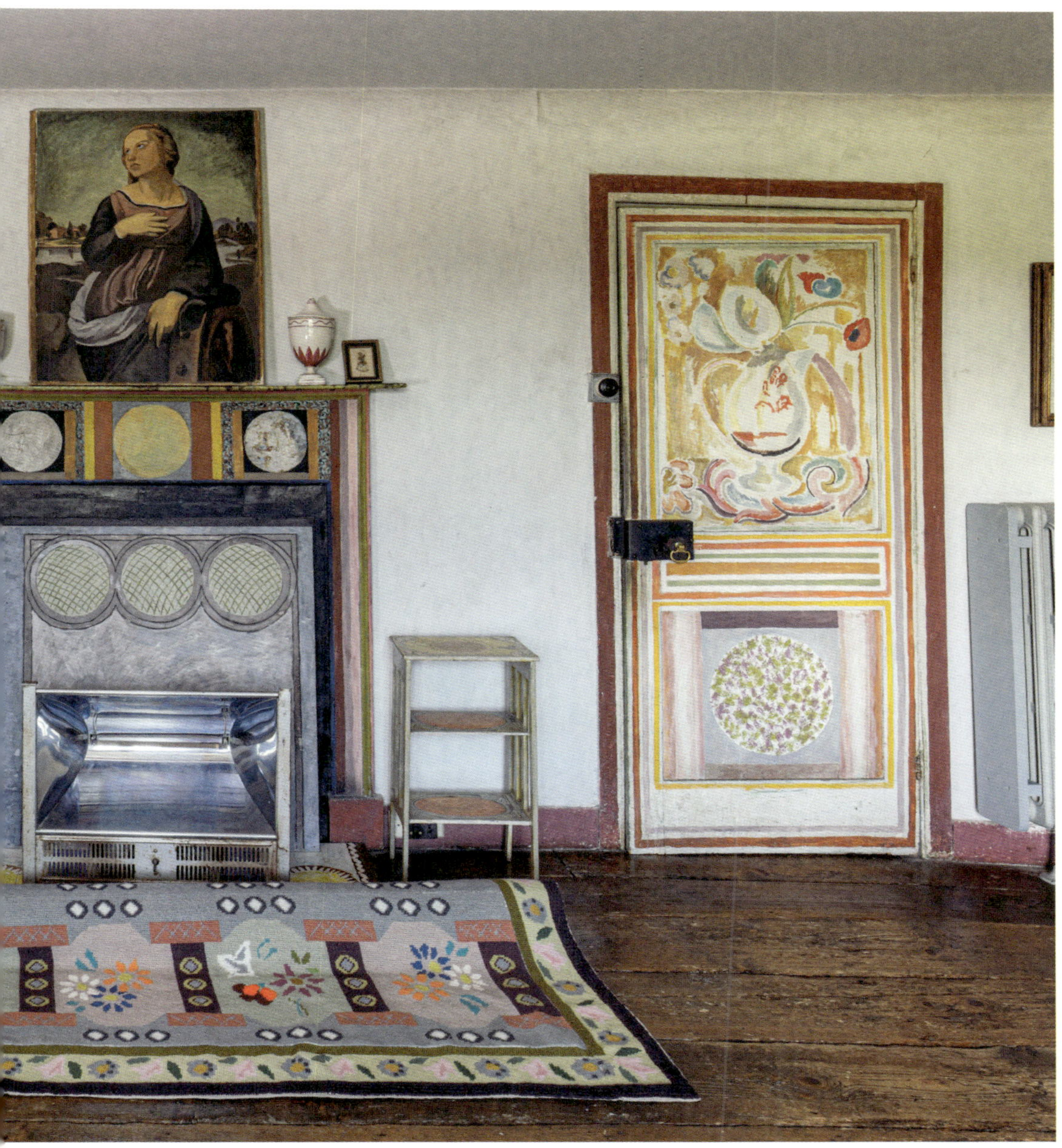

Painted in the interwar period, this fireplace combines Bell's signature circles, smaller dots and rows of cross-hatching, neater and more intricate than some of the later designs in the house. The three white circles are carefully shaded to give them a spherical appearance, while the rest is largely flat colour, dominated by the yellows, pinks and greys that would come to define the Charleston aesthetic. The house was infamously cold, especially in winter, and the elegance of Bell's design is balanced out by an unusual arrangement of bricks in this fireplace, devised by Fry to maximize the heat.

43. Fireplace decorations, 1925–6
Charleston

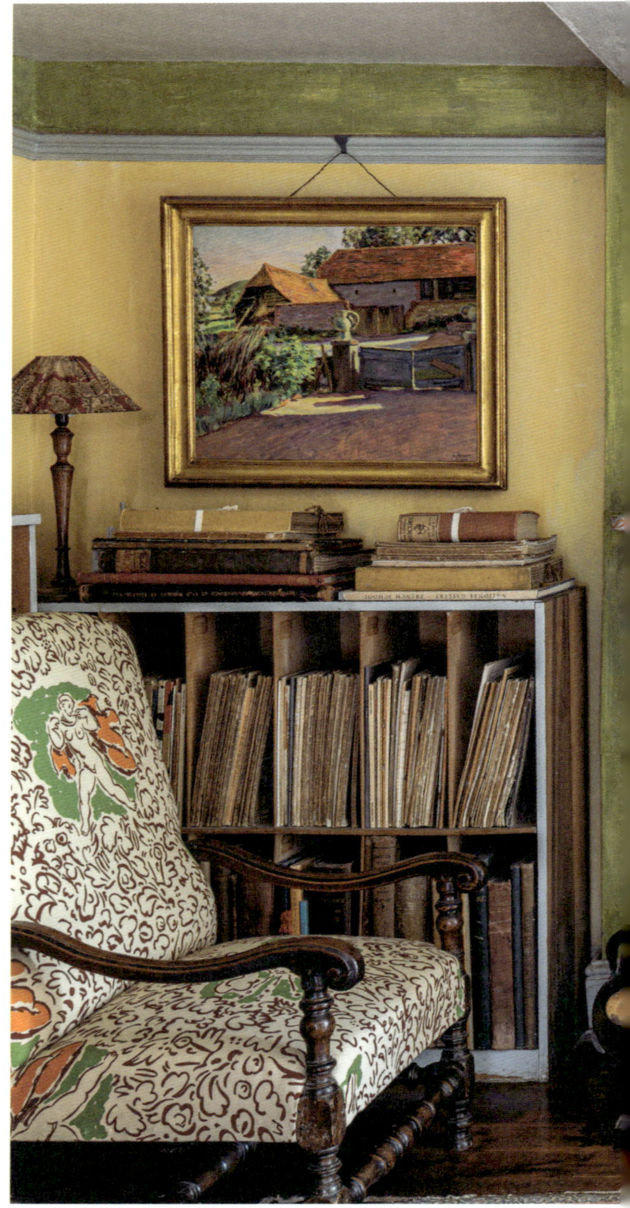

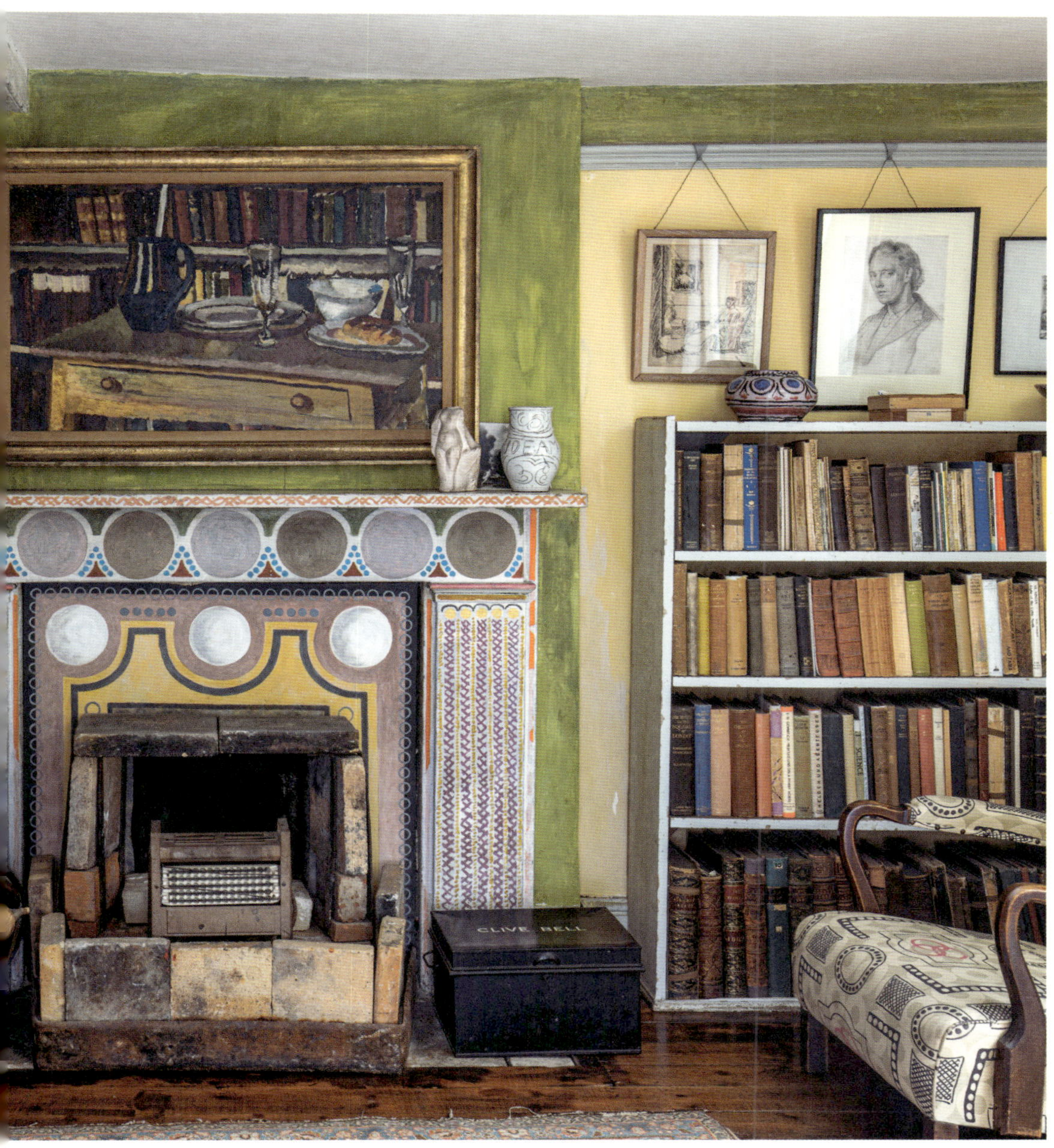
CLIVE BELL

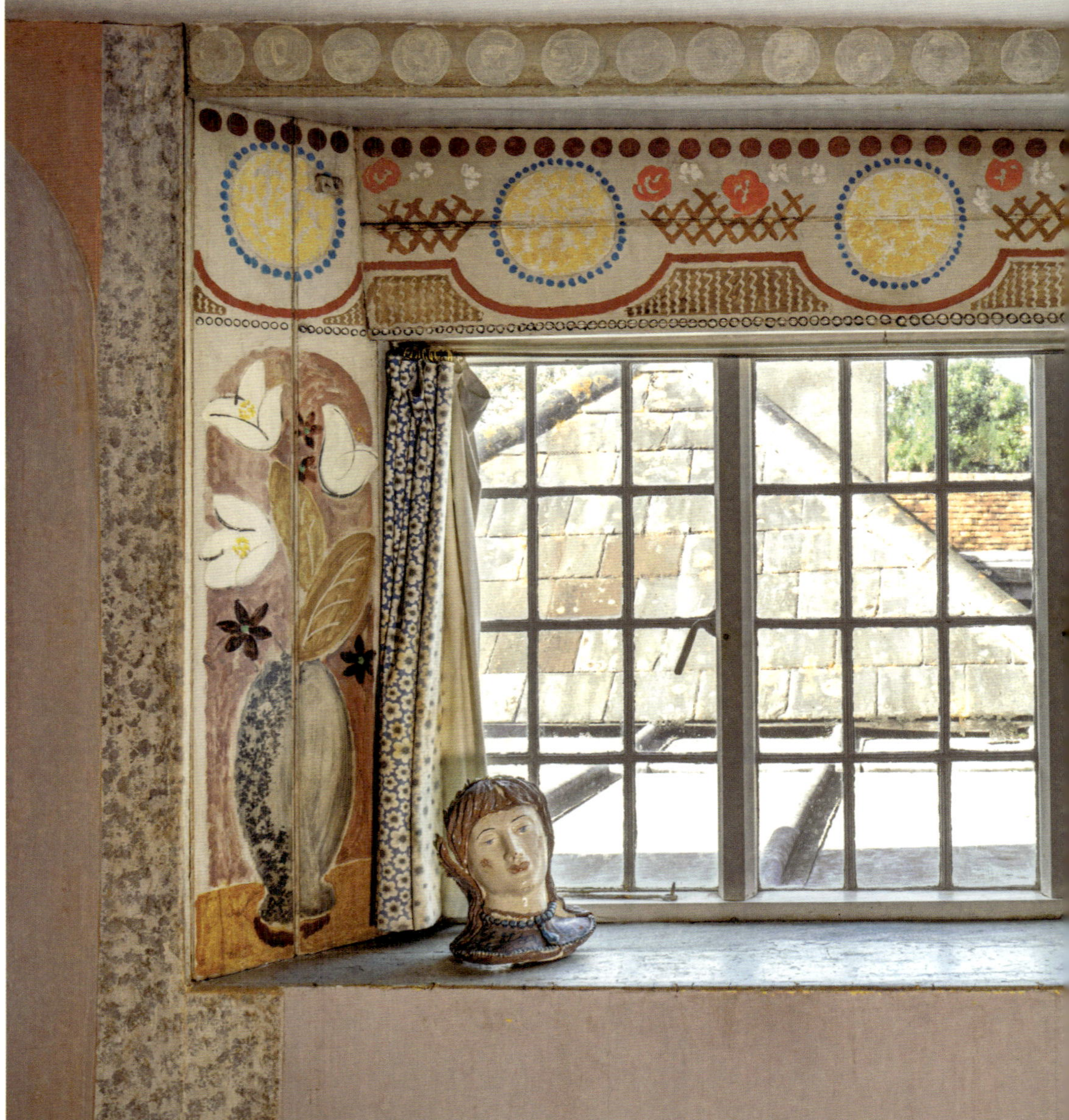

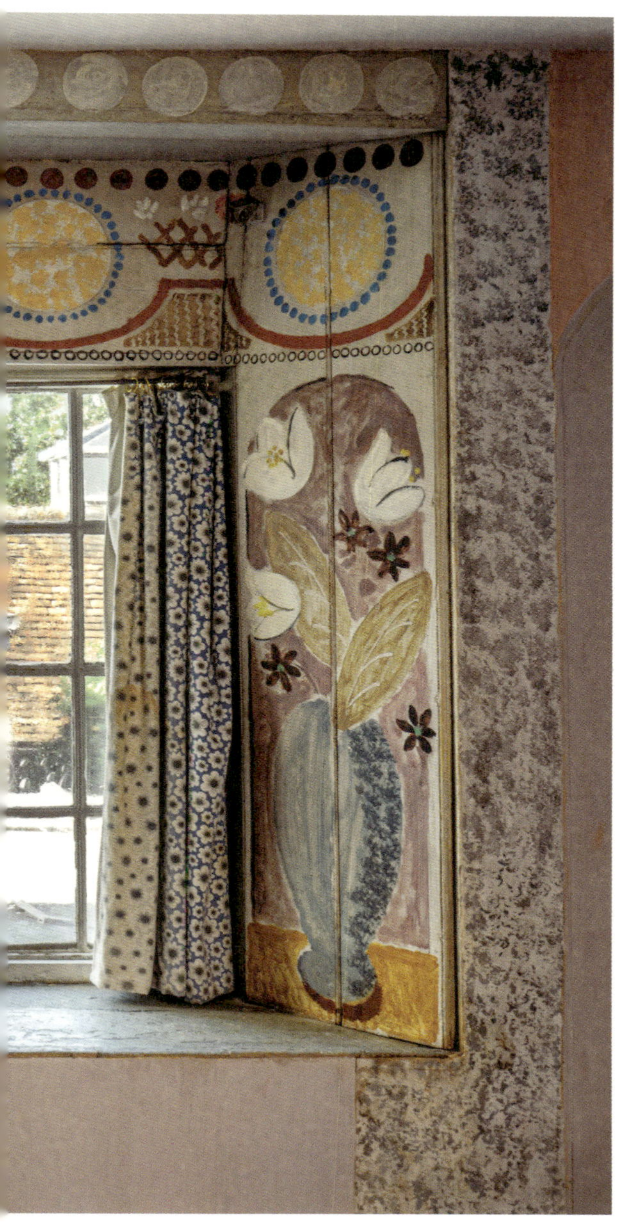

In these window decorations for the spare bedroom, Bell unified her combination of abstract and floral arrangement with both her colour scheme and her techniques. On both the abstract patterns across the lintel and the leaves in the floral designs, Bell has created line by scraping away wet paint from the surface to reveal the grey below. Her daubing of colour to create a marbled effect is used for both decoration and shading of the two vases, and even extends down the wall to either side.

44. Window decorations, 1936
Charleston

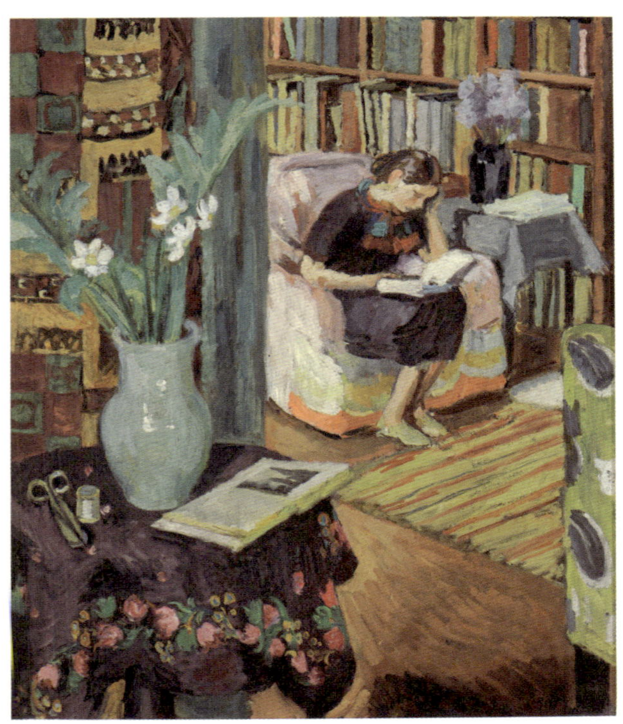

45. *Interior with the Artist's Daughter*, *c.* 1935–6
Oil on canvas, 73.7 × 61 cm
Charleston
(CHA/P/475)

Engrossed in a book, Angelica Bell is oblivious to her surroundings in this painting of her in the Charleston Studio, one of a series of works showing people within rooms that Bell created during this period. Here, pattern dominates every surface. The armchairs are covered in textiles designed by Grant for Allan Walton (1891–1948) (**63**) and a striped kilim lies beneath Angelica's feet. In the foreground, a table draped in an Italian fabric bears a book, scissors and thread, and a vase of narcissi that leads the eye up to another, more geometrically patterned textile.

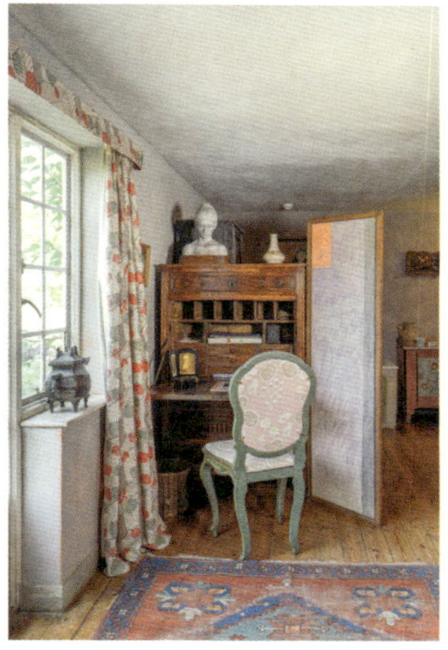

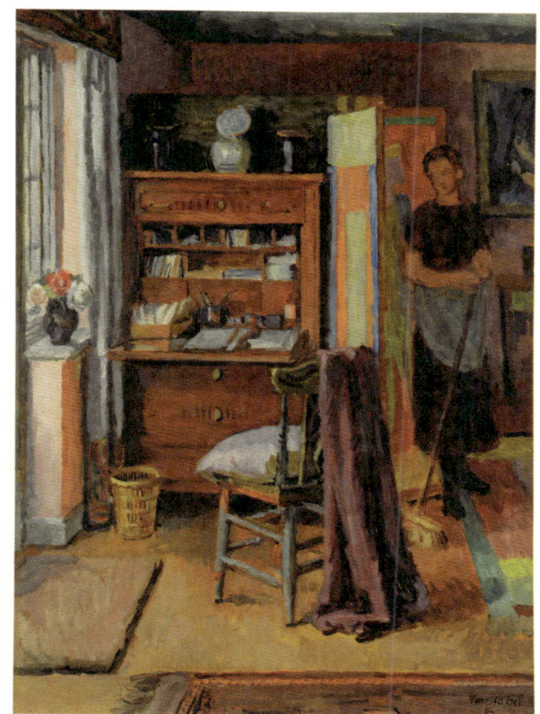

46. Vanessa Bell's bedroom at Charleston

47. *Interior with a Housemaid*, *c.* 1939
Oil on canvas, 74 × 54 cm
Williamson Art Gallery & Museum, Birkenhead
(BIKGM:2676)

Bell painted this scene shortly after making this room her bedroom. At centre is her writing desk, where she composed letters, with the chair pulled out as if recently abandoned. The titular housemaid is found to the right of the composition, on the other side of the Omega screen painted by Grant. The abstract geometric design on that screen, and the rug on the floor, cues the eye in to this picture's underlying structure of furniture and interior walls.

This large painting portrays Grace Higgens (1904–1983), housekeeper to Vanessa Bell for over 50 years, at work in the Charleston kitchen. Painted during the Second World War, at a time of rationing, the root vegetables and apples strewn across the table were most probably grown in the garden of Charleston by Grace's husband Walter. Incongruous to the traditional still life arrangement is the fridge, not yet a common convenience. The painting's monumental scale and earthy palette are both rare in Bell's work.

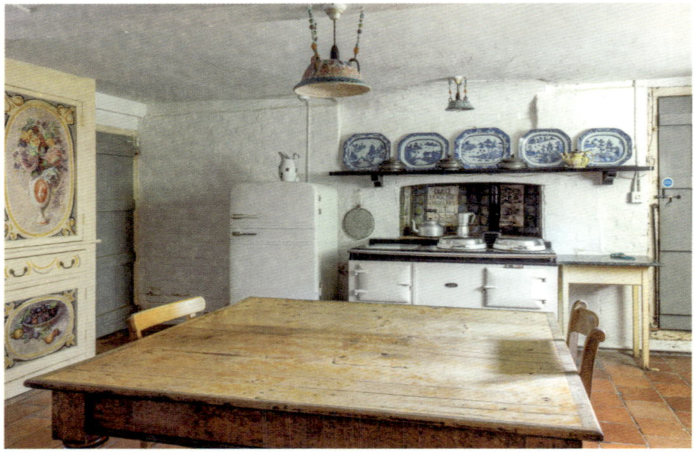

48. The kitchen at Charleston

49. *The Kitchen at Charleston*, *c.* 1943
Oil on canvas, 87.3 × 119.5 cm
Charleston
(CHA/P/174)

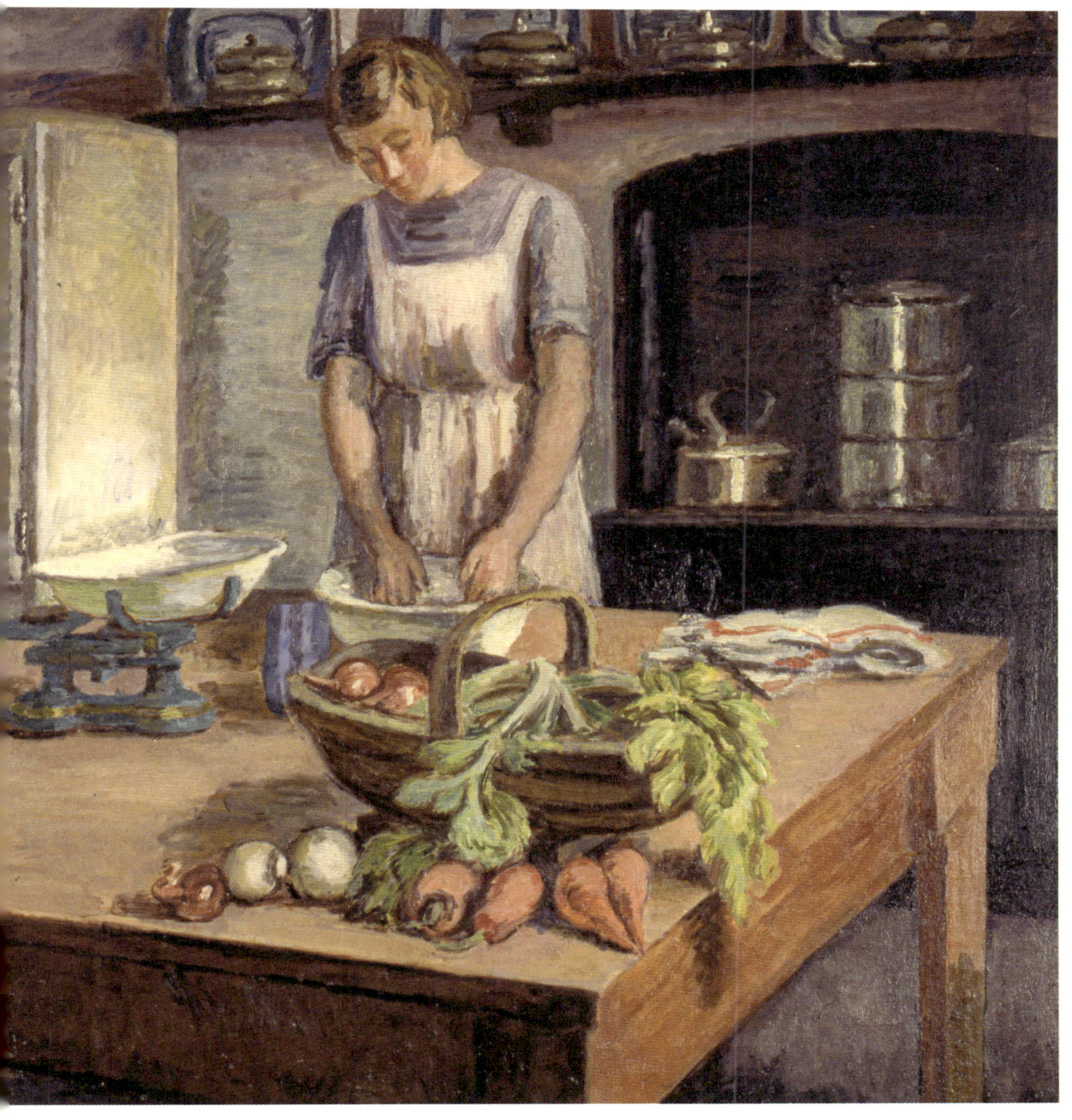

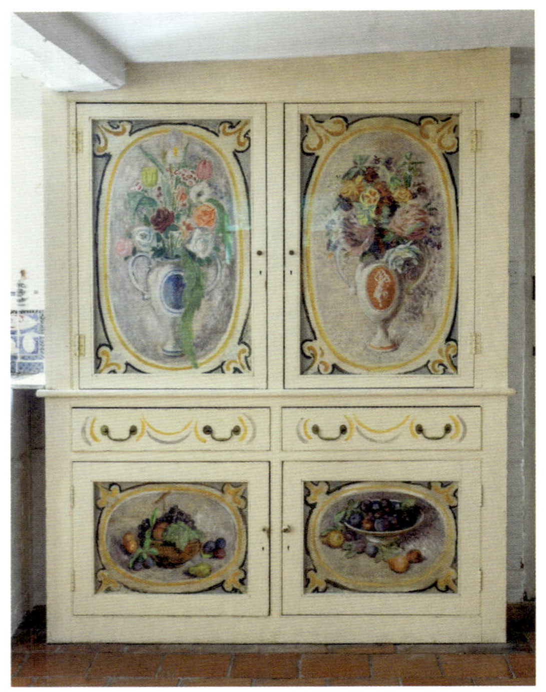

50. Kitchen cupboard decorations, *c.* 1950
Charleston

The two vases of flowers and bowls of fruit pictured on this kitchen cupboard overflow with bountiful supplies. Bell painted this around 1950, when wartime rationing was coming to an end. While many elements of these still lifes may have come from the Charleston garden, there is a palpable sense of pleasure in abundance. This is also evident in the lavish attention she pays to each bloom, in contrast to the stylized depictions of flowers she painted elsewhere in the house (41, 42, 44).

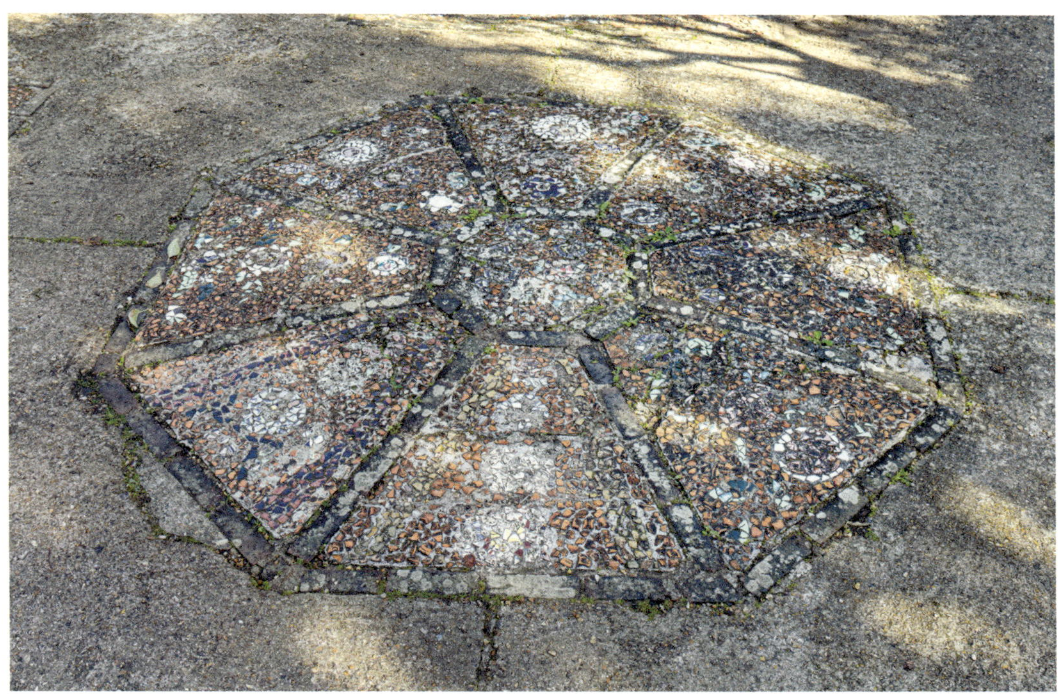

51. Mosaic set in concrete, 1946, with Quentin Bell and Duncan Grant, Charleston (CHA/SC/36)

The Charleston garden was first laid out by Roger Fry in 1918. As it developed, it benefited from the attention of a professional gardener, but the family remained involved as they loved growing flowers to paint. In 1946 Quentin, Bell's younger son, devised this 'piazza' at the bottom of the garden, featuring mosaics by Bell and Grant made from broken crockery. Some plates of Bell's own design, such as those made for Clarice Cliff (72), can be identified among the fragments. Bell also painted the ceramic tiles surrounding the nearby small pool around 1930, later replaced by copies painted by Quentin.

When Bell moved to Charleston in 1916, John Maynard Keynes moved into 46 Gordon Square. Together with Grant, she continued to decorate her former home, now occupied by a friend. On a cupboard, Bell depicted breakfast scenes in France, where she often travelled, and Turkey, which she had visited on holiday. The upper sections feature, respectively, Notre-Dame cathedral in Paris and the Hagia Sophia mosque in Istanbul, and two figures in stereotypical dress. Beneath are shown breakfast trays, each with the country's distinctive design of coffee pot. On an accompanying cupboard, Grant depicted St. Paul's Cathedral, London, and St. Peter's, Rome, accompanied by English and Italian figures and breakfasts.

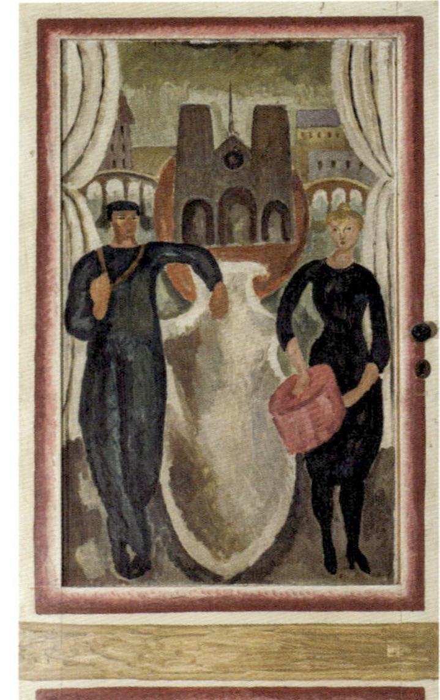

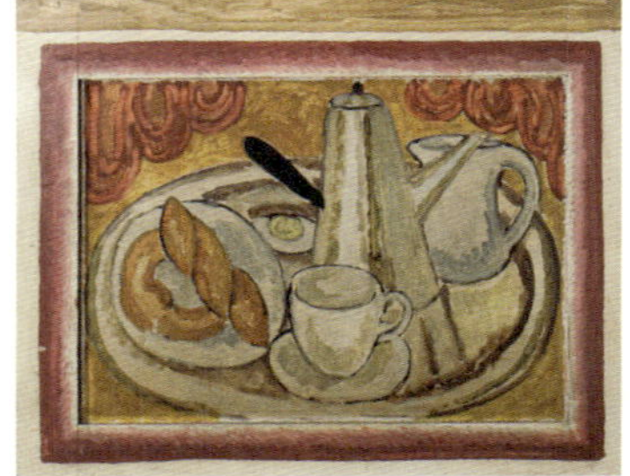

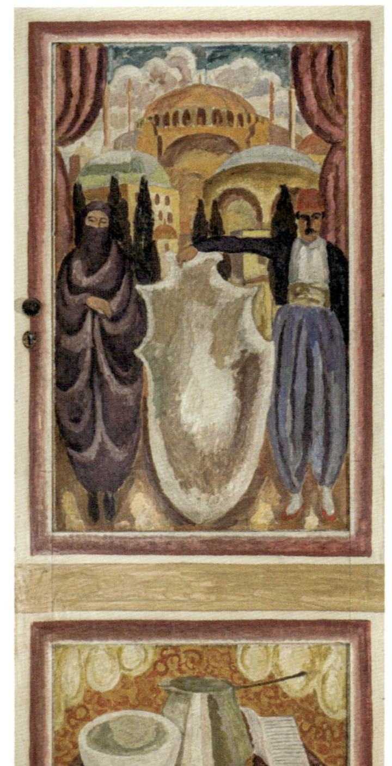

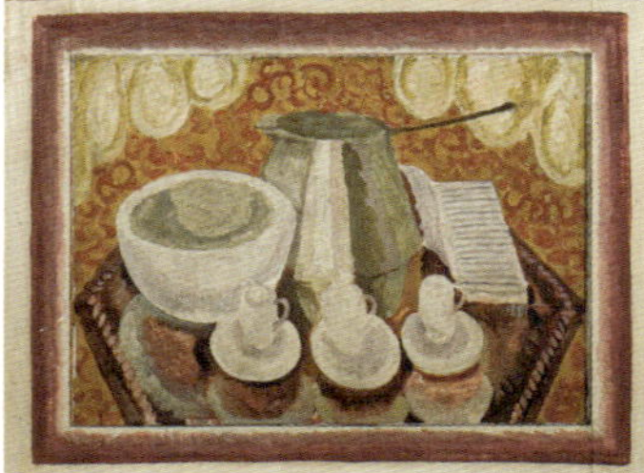

52. Cupboard door decorations for 46 Gordon Square, *c.* 1921, with Duncan Grant
Gouache on wood
King's College Cambridge

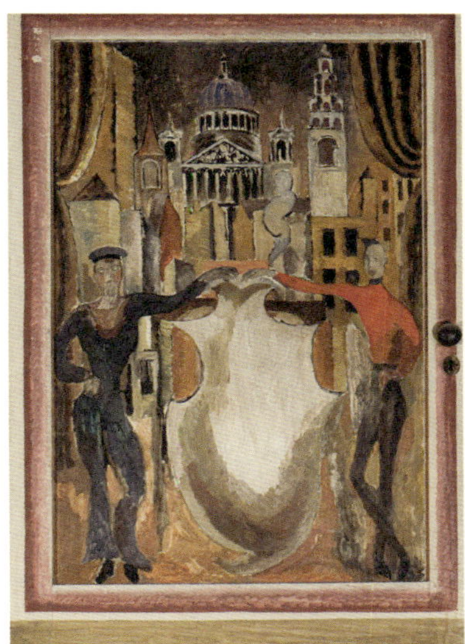
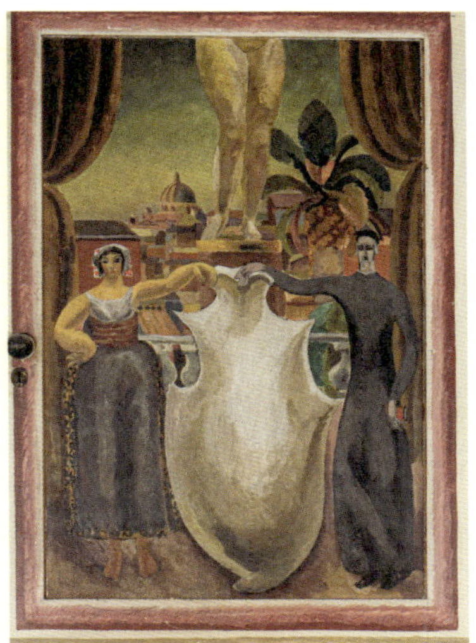
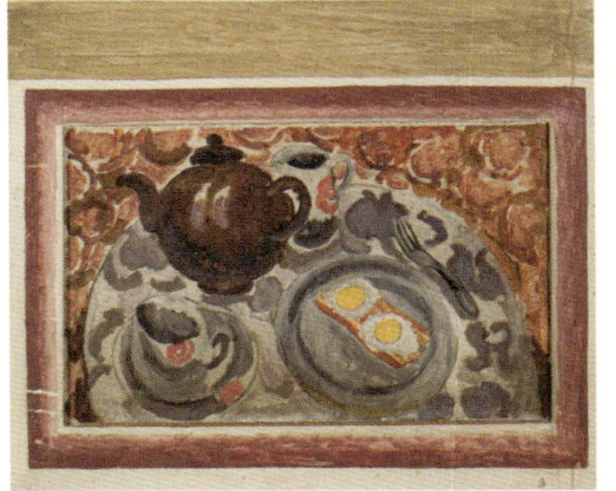
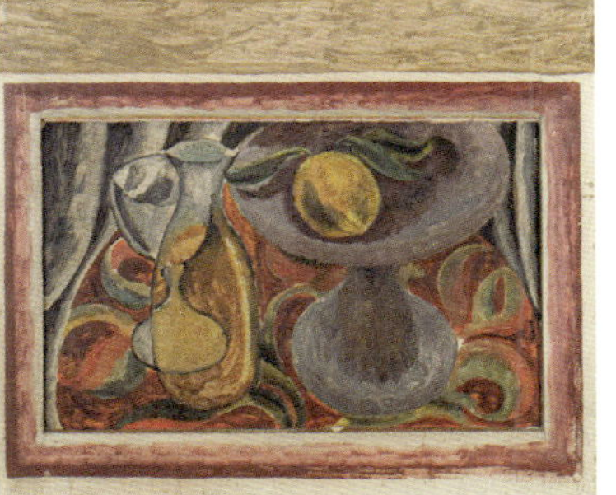

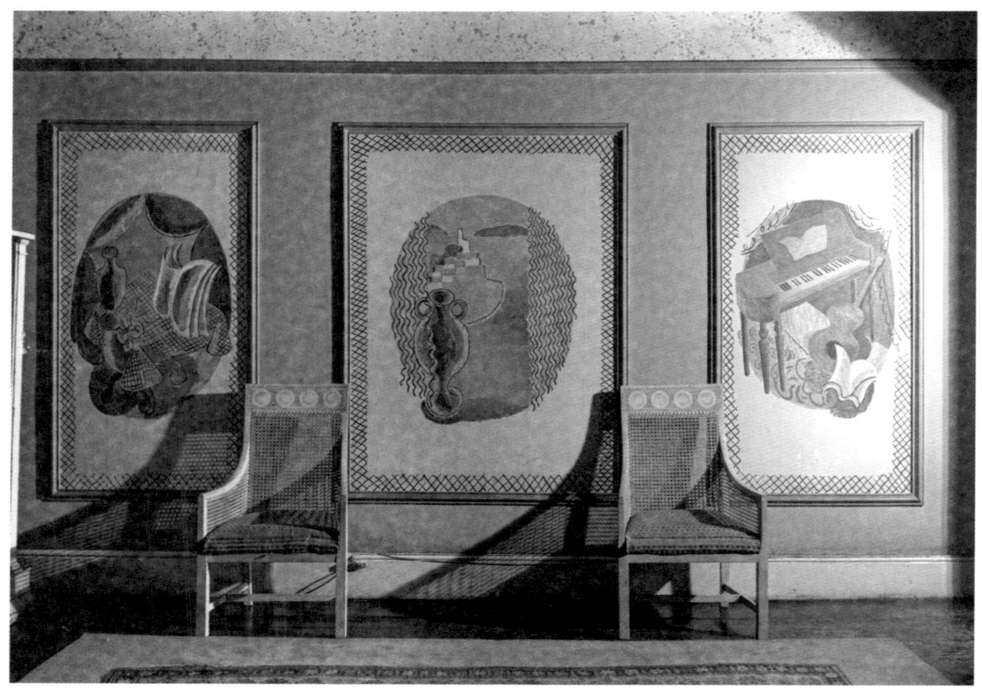

53. Decorations for 52 Tavistock Square, 1924, with Duncan Grant
Black-and-white negative, taken in 1930 by Dell & Wainwright
Architectural Press Archive/RIBA Collections (RIBA52388)

54. *Virginia Woolf*, 1934
Oil on canvas, 94 × 74 cm
Charleston
(LL/CHA/P/314)

Bell and Grant decorated the living room of Virginia and Leonard Woolf's new London home with three still life panels and a frieze of swirling lines above the picture rail. The house was destroyed by a bomb in 1940, but a painting by Bell (54), a photograph by Gisèle Freund (**fig. 9**) and a description in *Vogue* illuminate its avant-garde colour scheme: 'The walls are pale dove-gray, the panels glossy white with tomato-red borders and oval "fonds" alternately in sienna pink and maple yellow. The subjects are painters in umbers, browns, and white, with touches of lettuce-green. The narrow frieze is in wallpaper with "écriture" of subdued violet on white and brown yellow.'[37]

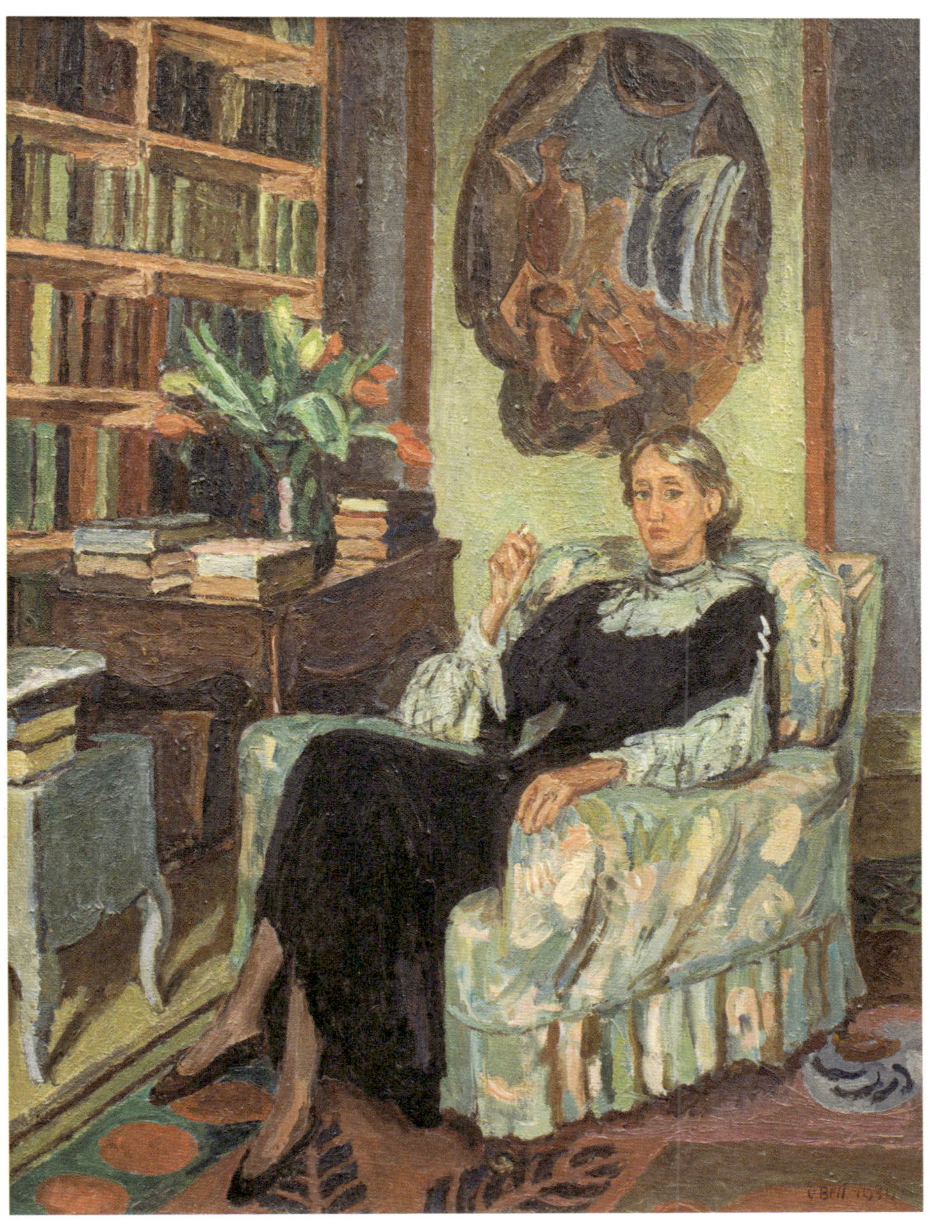

After moving to Bloomsbury to be closer to his friends, the writer Raymond Mortimer sought out Bell and Grant as decorators for his small flat. Bell painted an enormous canvas that stretched from floor to ceiling with an illusionistic garden scene with a fountain and musical instruments, framed by theatrical red curtains (opposite page, right). Grant painted smaller canvases to go over the doors (right), their complementary compositions evident in a photograph (55; below). Bell's sketchbooks show that she considered a simpler fountain, or having a statue instead, and that she also toyed with an illusionistic balustrade to cordon off this idyllic space (56; opposite page, left).

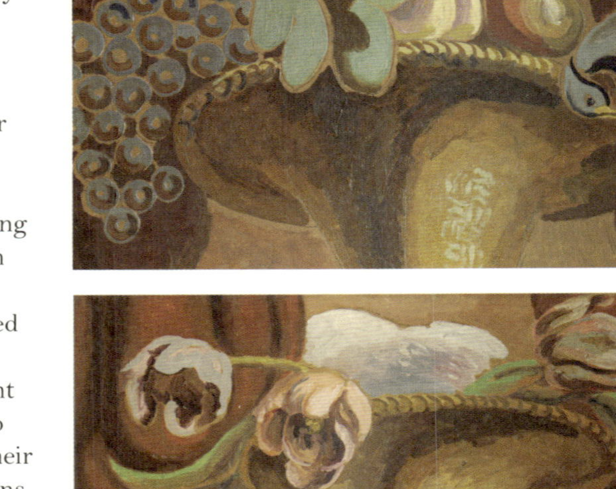

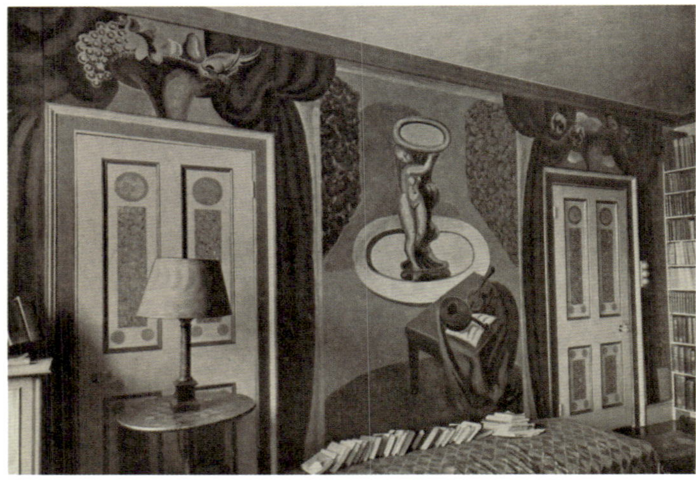

55. Raymond Mortimer's home at 6 Gordon Place, illustrated in Dorothy Todd and Raymond Mortimer, *The New Interior Decoration* (1929)
Victoria and Albert Museum, London (V&A NAL: L.1118-1929)

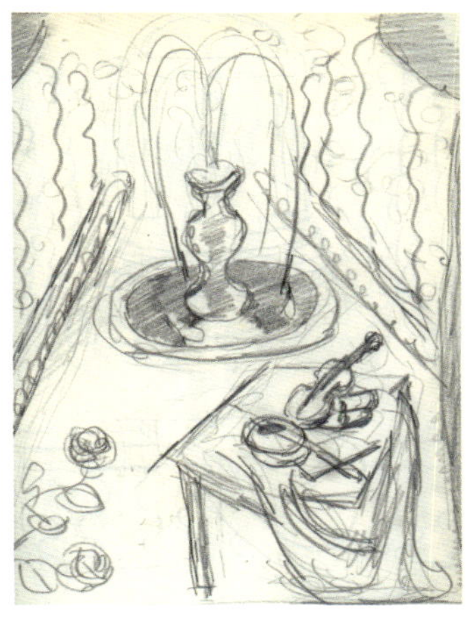

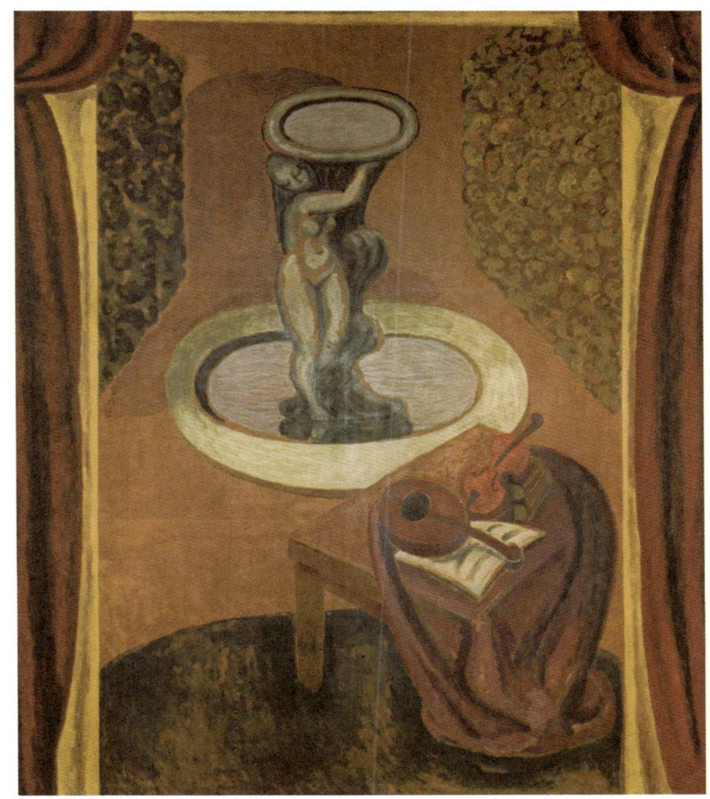

56. Sketchbook, early 1920s
Pencil on paper
Charleston
(CHA/P/419)

57. Decorations for 6 Gordon Place, 1925, with Duncan Grant
Oil on canvas, opposite, top: 50.8 × 112 cm; opposite, middle: 50.2 × 113 cm; above, right: 263 × 224.4 cm
Victoria and Albert Museum, London
(V&A: P.2-1953, P.5-1953, P.6-1953)
Given by Raymond Mortimer, 1953

When the Hutchinsons moved from Hammersmith (see p. 26) to Regent's Park, they invited Bell and Grant to decorate their new home. Grant's watercolour design for the drawing room shows many of the pair's signature motifs, including a vertiginous flower arrangement, faux-marbled door panels, and illusionistic swags of fabric. In keeping with the house's Georgian architecture, Bell and Grant conjured up a suitably 'classical feeling', praised by *Vogue*.[38] The photograph in that magazine, which shows Bell's panels above the bookcases, reveals how their whimsical designs were transferred to the elegantly proportioned panels.

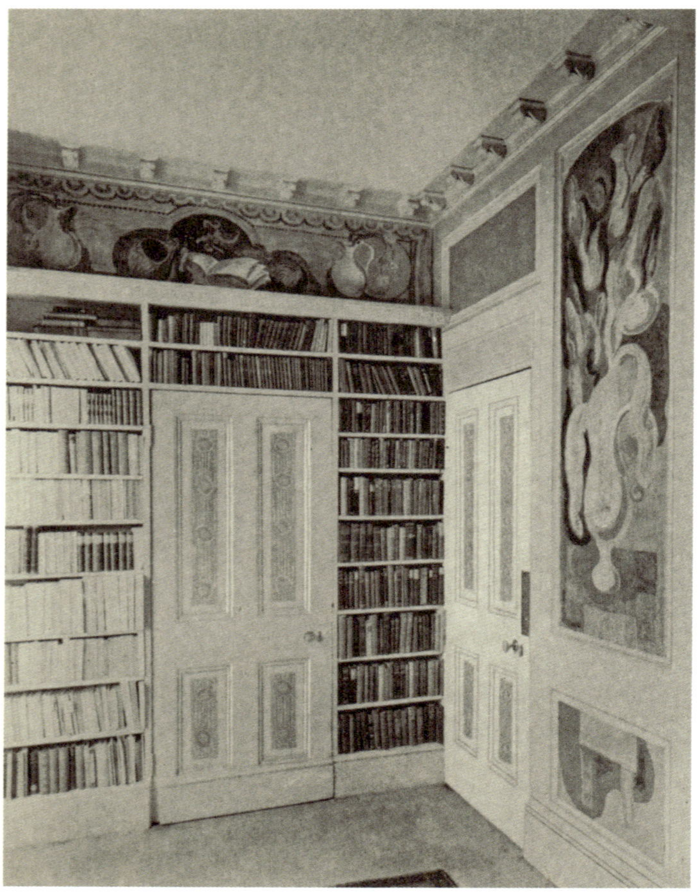

58. Decorations for 3 Albert Gate, London, illustrated in Dorothy Todd and Raymond Mortimer, *The New Interior Decoration* (1929)
Victoria and Albert Museum, London
(V&A NAL: L.1118-1929)

59. Duncan Grant, design for 3 Albert Gate, 1926
Watercolour on paper, 37.4 × 24.1 cm
Victoria and Albert Museum, London
(V&A: E.159-1982)

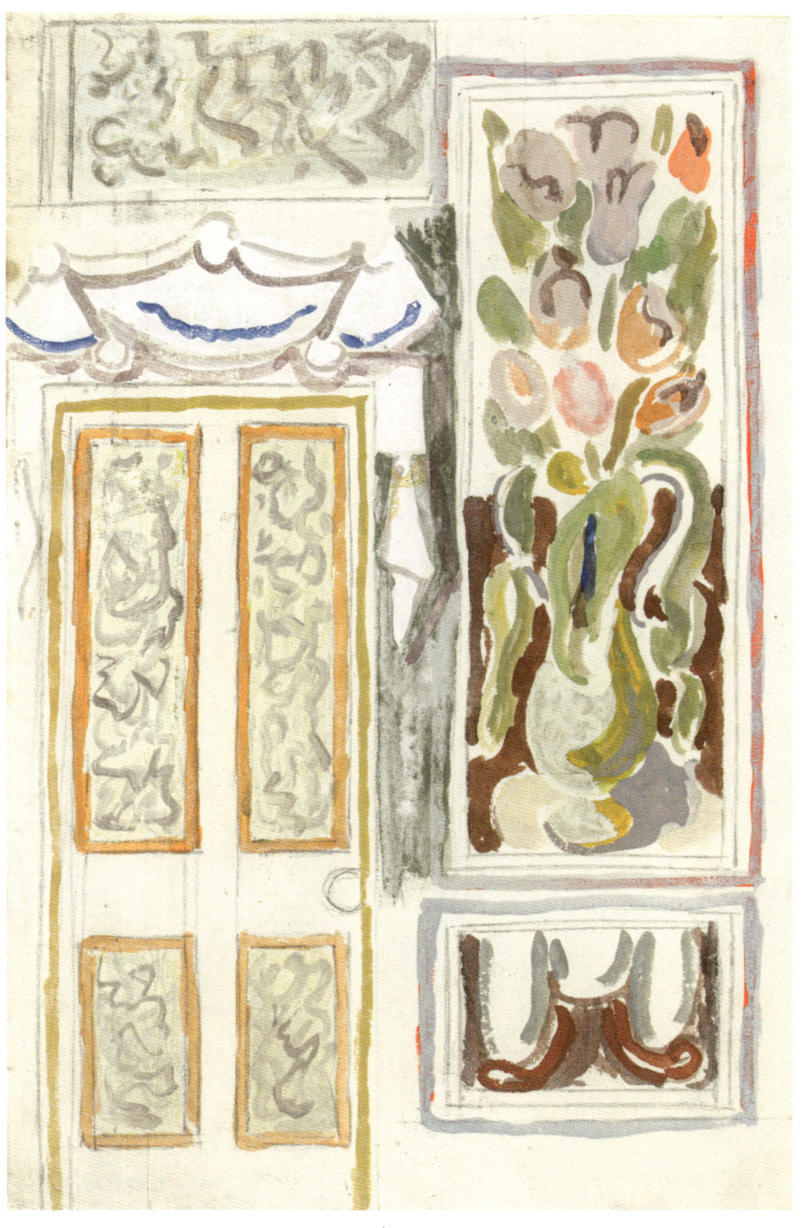

In 1930 the editor of the *Architectural Review* launched a competition to design the apartment of Lord Benbow, a Clydeside shipbuilder who wanted his London apartment designed by modernist artists. Bell devised a scheme with sporting motifs, collaborating with Grant for painted panels, Humphrey Slater (1905–1958) for carpets and fabrics, John Skeaping (1901–1980) for sculpture and Robert Medley (1905–1994) for furniture and light fittings. Bell's colour scheme won her praise, but her design was described as treating the layout of the room as a comparative irrelevancy. Bell came third, with Paul Nash taking second prize and Raymond McGrath (1903–1977) the victor.

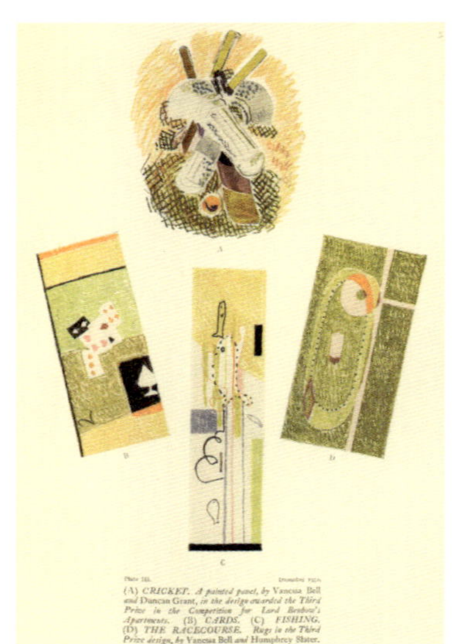

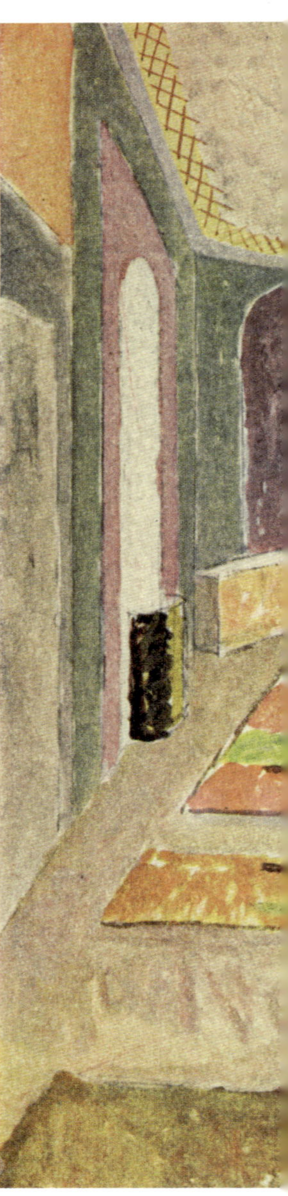

60. Design for painted panel, 1930, with Duncan Grant, and rugs, with Humphrey Slater, illustrated in *Architectural Review*
Victoria and Albert Museum, London
(V&A NAL: 38041800903049)

61. Design for Lord Benbow's apartment, 1930, illustrated in *Architectural Review*
Victoria and Albert Museum, London
(V&A NAL: 380418009030499)

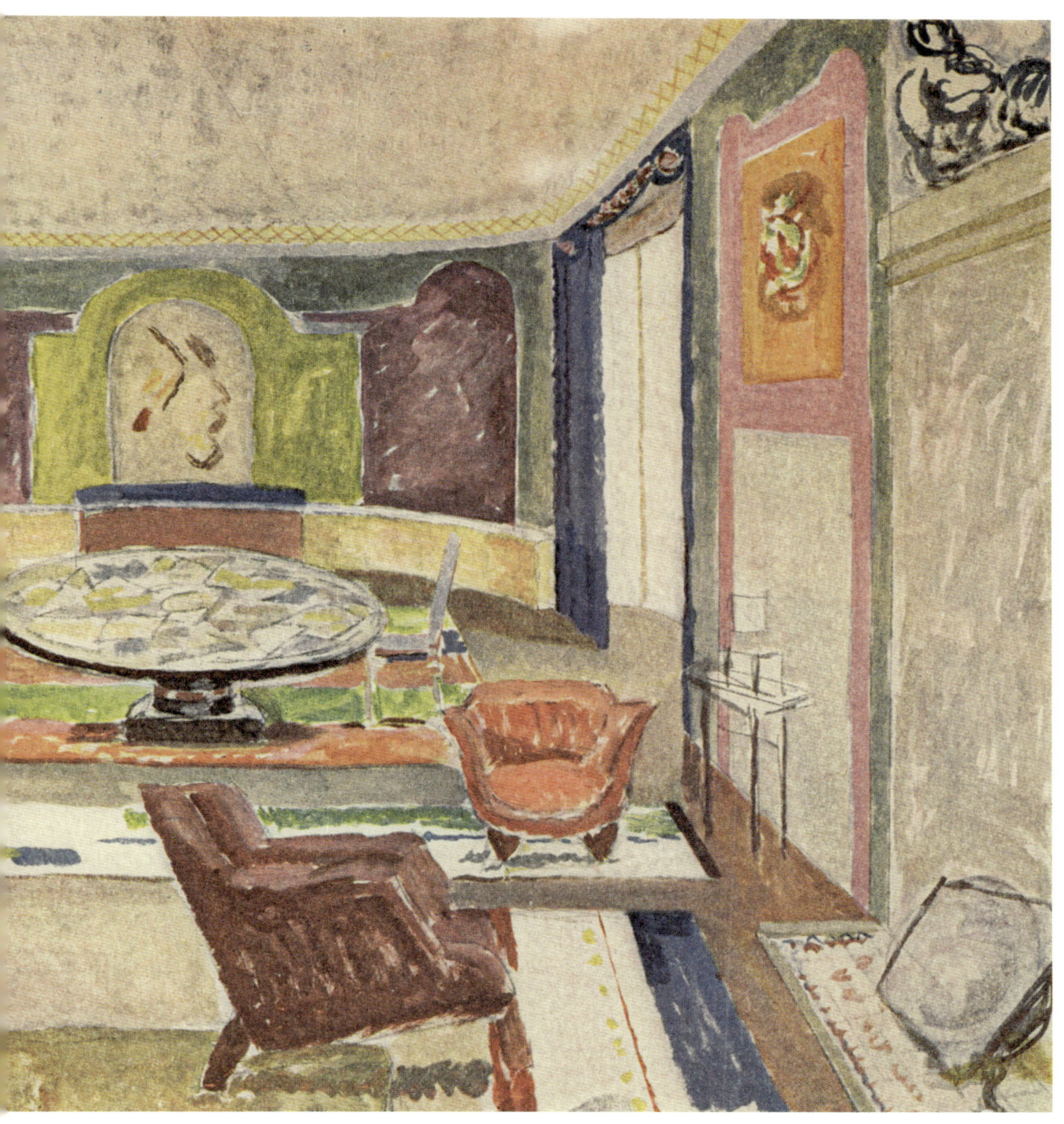

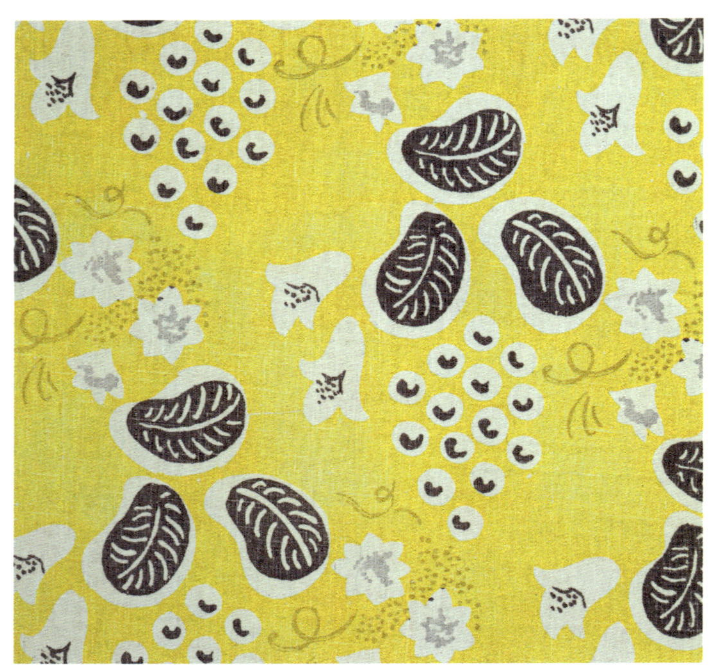

62. Duncan Grant, 'Grapes' textile, 1932, made by Allan Walton Textiles
Printed linen
Victoria and Albert Museum, London
(V&A: Circ.236B-1935)

63. Music Room installed at Alex Reid and Lefevre Gallery, 1932, with Duncan Grant, illustrated in Derek Patmore, *Colour Schemes for the Modern Home* (1933)
Victoria and Albert Museum, London
(V&A NAL: L.2620-1933)

With the financial support of Virginia Woolf, Bell and Grant created this room inspired by classical music, including Bach, Mozart, Debussy, Chopin and Stravinsky, for a London art gallery. It featured many of their hallmark painted screens and tiled hearths, and circles, swags and floral arrangements abound. Some elements indicate their latest collaborations: the curtains and upholstery used the 'Grapes' textile designed by Grant for the artist and designer Allan Walton (**62**), and the ceramics were those made with potter Phyllis Keyes (1881–1968) (**64**, **65**). Nonetheless, the design was not in keeping with the modernist preference for simplicity, and this would be their last major domestic scheme.

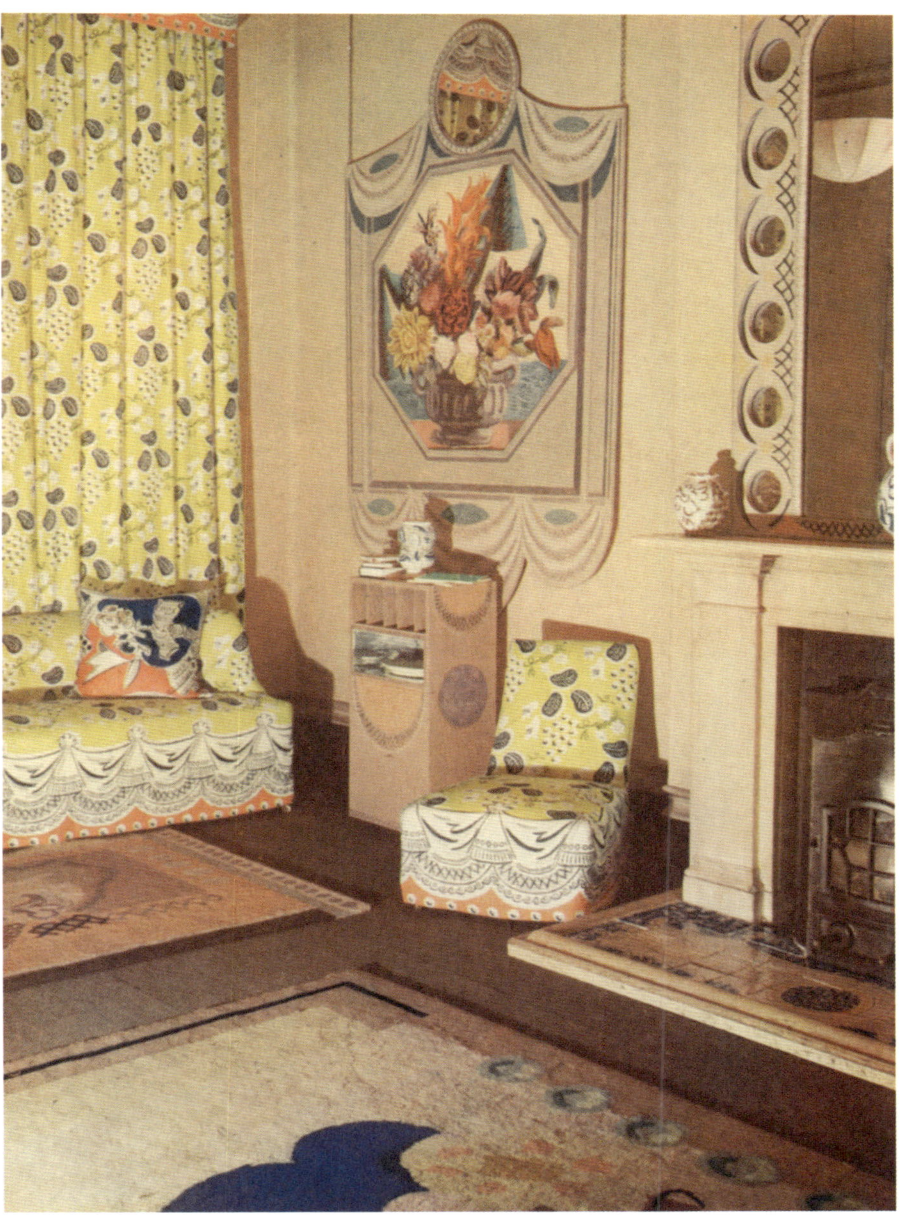

These two vases were made by potter Phyllis Keyes and decorated by Bell. They met in 1931 and Keyes collaborated with Bloomsbury artists throughout the decade. Seemingly self-taught, Keyes had a workshop and a kiln on Warren Street and sold her wares through the interior design and furnishings store, Heal's. Now held at Charleston, one of these vases was featured in the 1932 Music Room (**63**). The vases' curvaceous forms and floral motifs are quite different to the Omega ceramics made in the 1910s, but the stylized single sunflower of the V&A vase resembles the window decorations Bell undertook at Charleston in that decade (**41**).

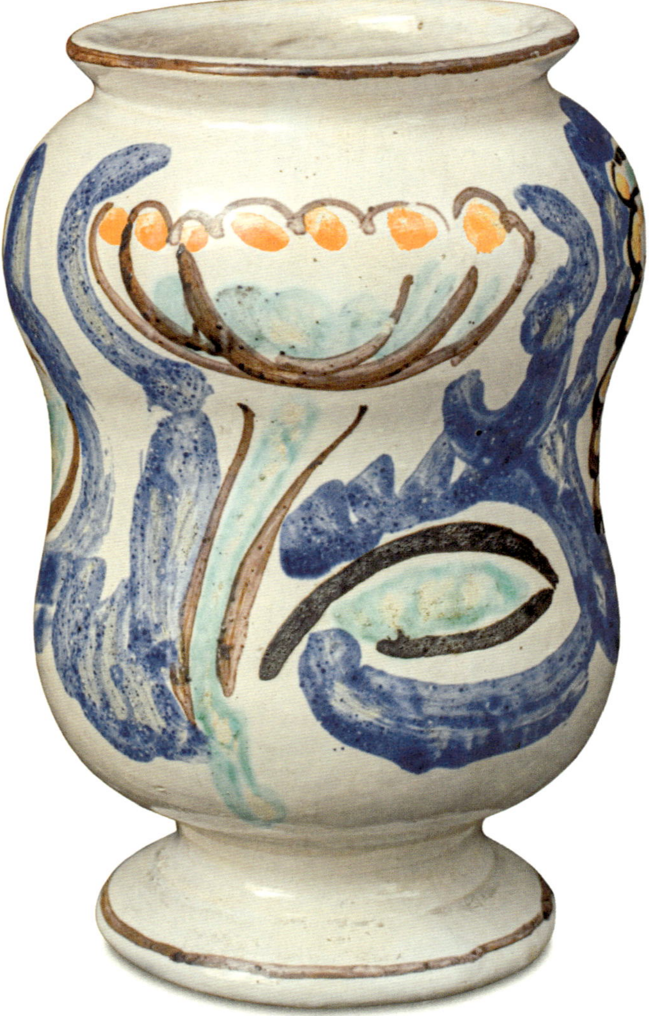

64. Music Room vase, 1932,
thrown by Phyllis Keyes and painted
by Vanessa Bell
Tin-glazed earthenware,
painted in colours
Charleston
(CHA/C/181)

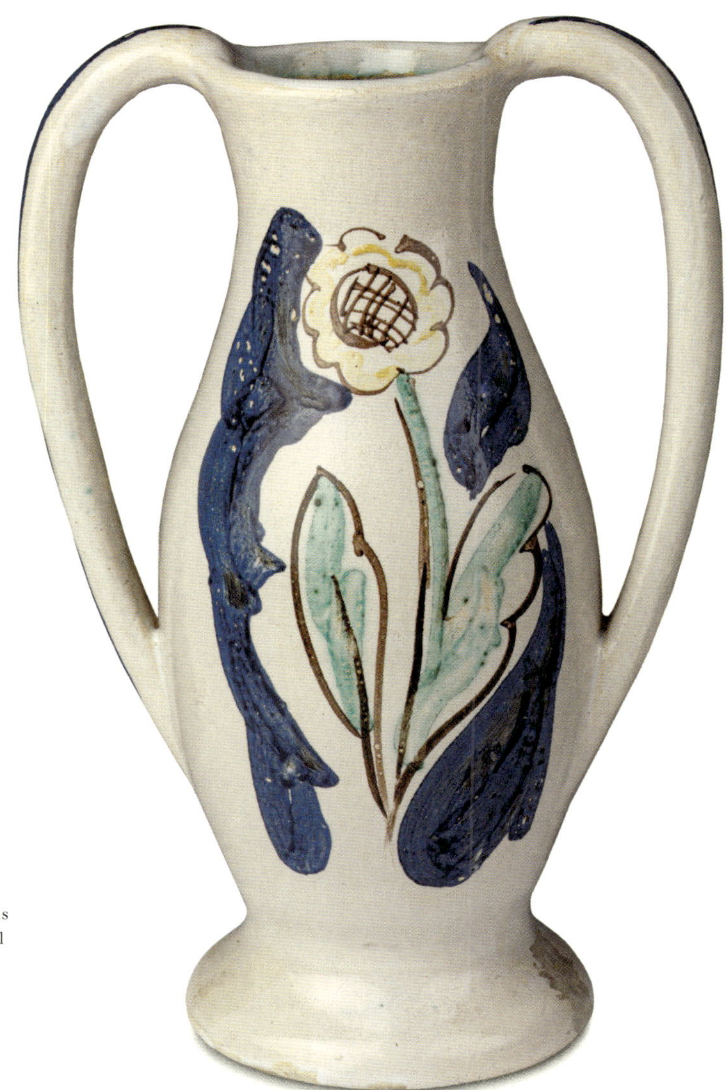

65. Vase, *c.* 1932, thrown by Phyllis Keyes and painted by Vanessa Bell
Tin-glazed earthenware, painted in colours
Victoria and Albert Museum, London (V&A: Misc.2:136-1934)
Given by Mrs Margaret H. Armitage (née Bulley)

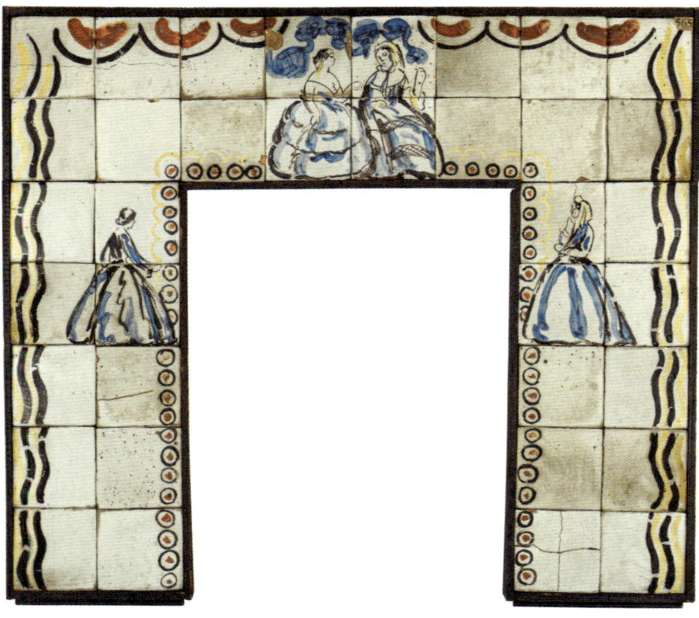

66. Fireplace, 1920s
Tin-glazed earthenware, painted in colours
Victoria and Albert Museum, London (V&A: Misc.2:61-1934)
Given by Mrs Margaret H. Armitage (née Bulley)

This fireplace features Bell's characteristic decoration of circles and waves at the inner and outer edges but, more unusually, also includes figures in historical costume. The voluminous blue dresses themselves appear eighteenth-century, yet the loose drawing of these four women owes more to illustrations found in the fashion magazines Bell read, such as *Vogue*. This was one of three Bell and Grant tiled fireplaces pictured in Todd and Mortimer's book *The New Interior Decoration* (1929), yet it was not shown installed in a home, so little is known about whether or not it was designed for a specific interior.

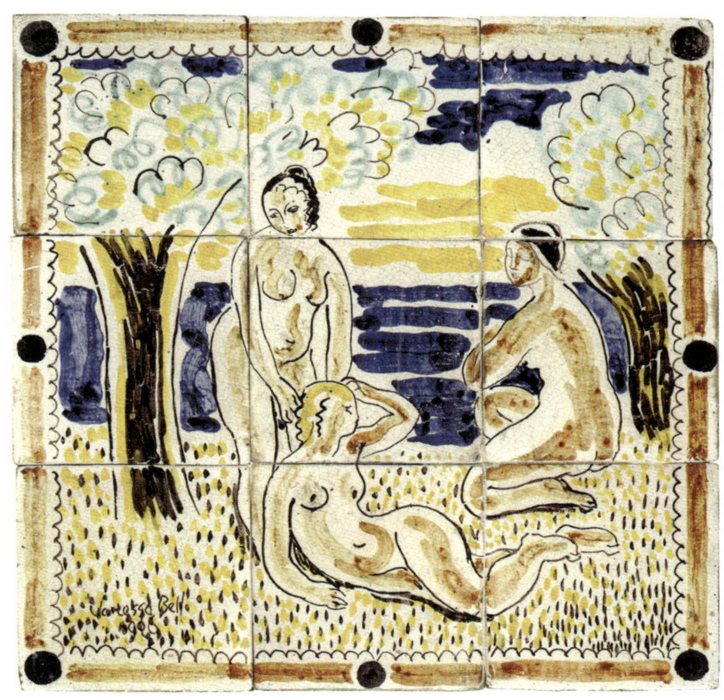

67. Tile panel, 1926
Tin-glazed earthenware,
painted in colours
Victoria and Albert Museum, London
(V&A: C.22-1999)

Tile panels offered Bell a middle ground between painting and decoration. In this idyllic scene of bathers in a landscape, she created stylized outlines of the figures, loosely rendered the trees, sea and sky, and used short vertical strokes for the area of land, perhaps grass, perhaps sand, on which they stand, lie and kneel. These elements demonstrate her continuing interest in the work of Henri Matisse and her active participation in creating ceramics in the 1920s, the decade between her collaborations with the Omega Workshops and Phyllis Keyes.

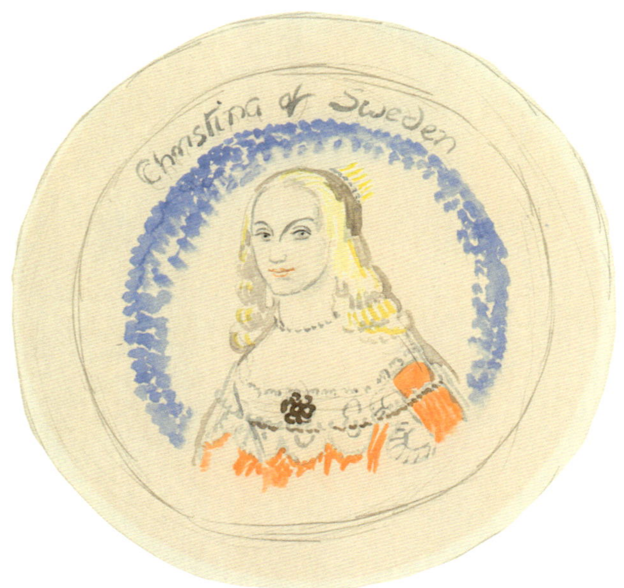

68. Design for Christina of Sweden plate, 1932–3
Pencil and watercolour on paper, dia. 25.5 cm
Victoria and Albert Museum, London (V&A: E.1052-1992)

The commission for this dinner service came from Kenneth and Jane Clark (1903–1983; 1902–1976), but the theme was chosen by Bell and Grant who, alongside queens, included women of letters, beauties, dancers and actresses, ranging from Helen of Troy to Marian Bergeron, the winner of the 1933 Miss America pageant. Bell declared that the theme of famous women 'ought to please the feminists' while Kenneth Clark described it as 'Bloomsbury asserting its status as a matriarchy'.[39] The dinner service was in private hands for more than 80 years, but known through designs such as this.

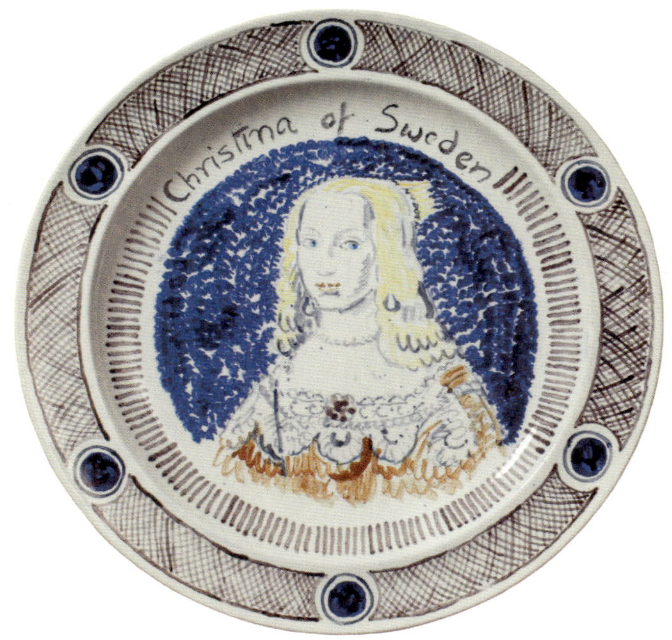

69. Christina of Sweden plate, 1932–3
Hand-painted on a Wedgwood
blank earthenware plate
Charleston
(CHA/C/714)

70. *The Famous Women Dinner Service*,
1932–4, with Duncan Grant
Hand-painted on Wedgwood
blank earthenware plates
Charleston
(CHA/P/684-733)

Christina, who ruled Sweden from 1632 to 1654, is one of twelve queens to appear on the Famous Women dinner service painted by Bell and Grant. The portraits were based on existing images, a seventeenth-century print in the case of Christina, and planned in watercolour (**68**). When Bell and Grant painted their designs onto 50 blank plates purchased from Wedgwood, they added four different decorative borders (**70**). Christina's inclusion may have been prompted by the 1933 biopic starring Greta Garbo, who is also portrayed on a plate.

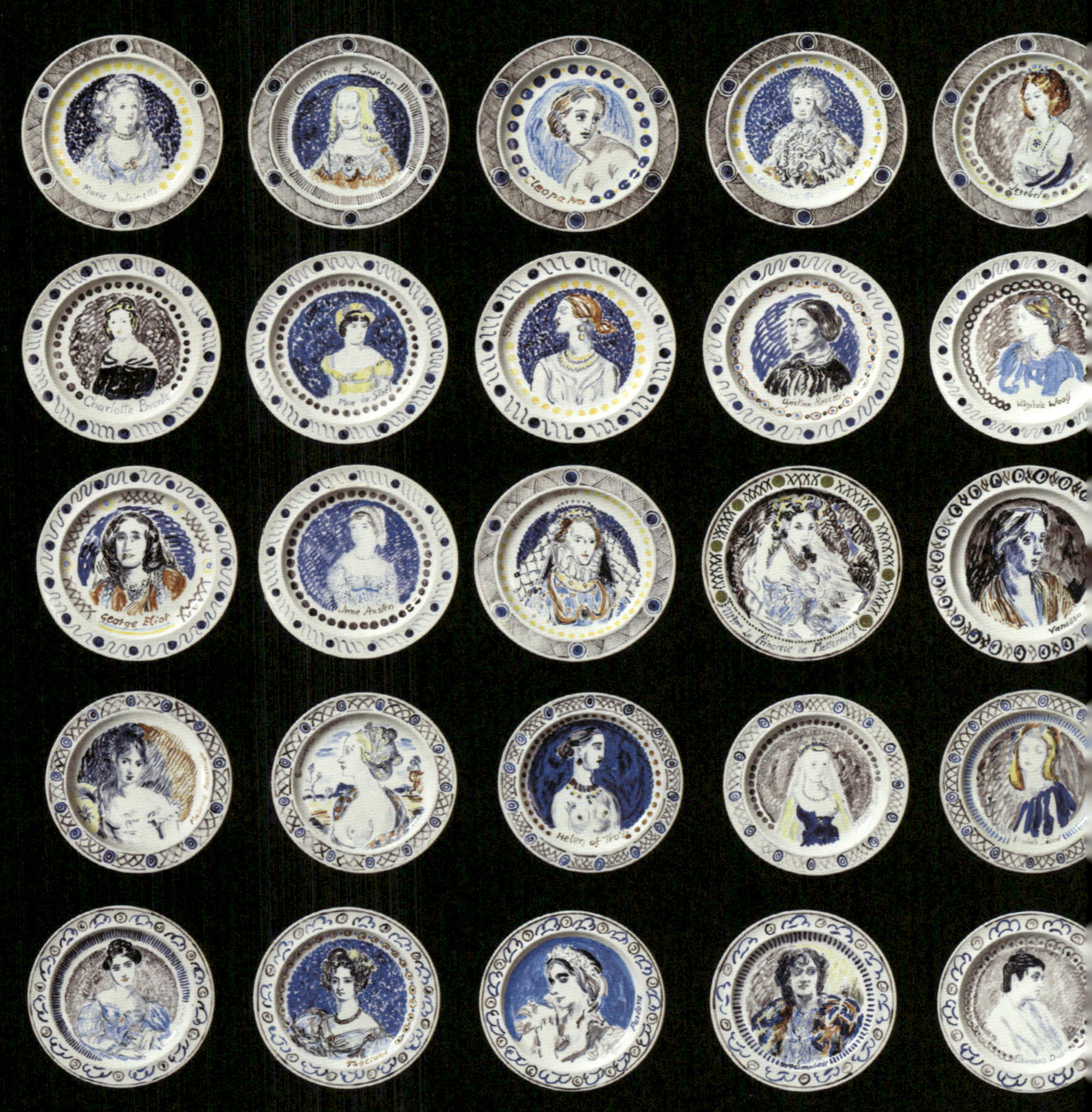

Marie Antoinette
Christina of Sweden
Cleopatra
Jezebel
Charlotte Bronte
Mme de Staël
Christina Rossetti
Virginia Woolf
George Eliot
Jane Austen
Princesse de Metternich
Vanessa
Helen of Troy
Taglioni

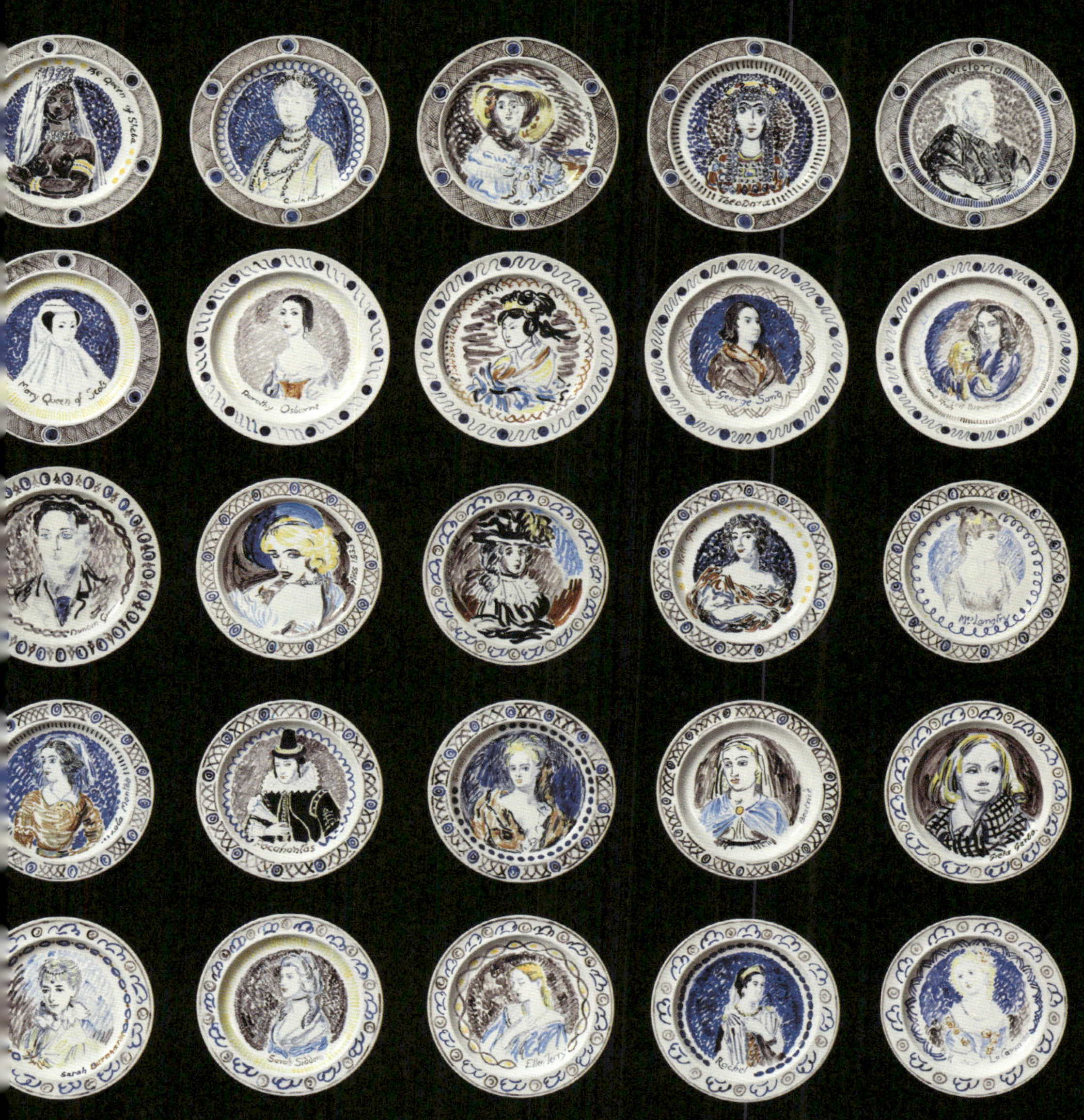
Theodora
Victoria
Mary Queen of Scots
Dorothy Osborne
George Sand
Pocahontas
Beatrice
Greta Garbo
Sarah Siddons
Ellen Terry
Rachel

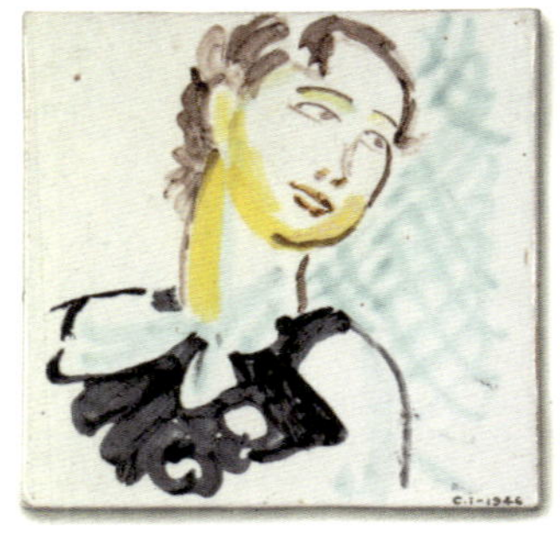
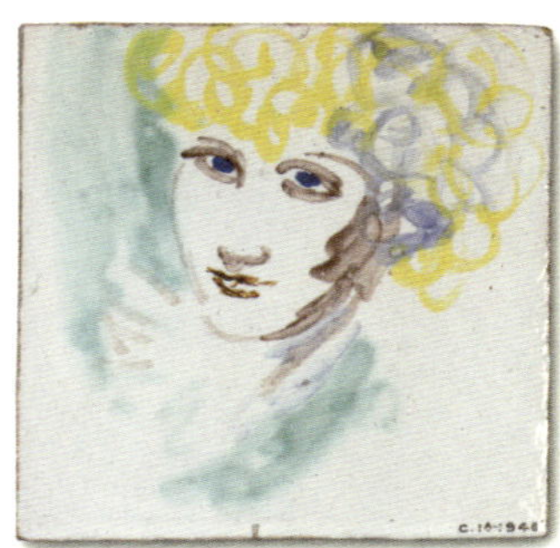
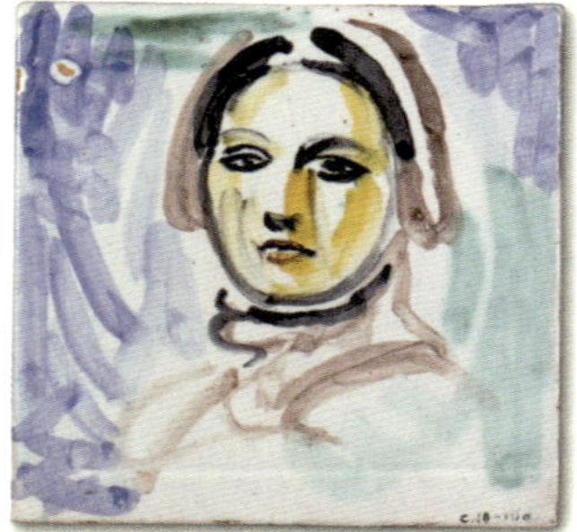
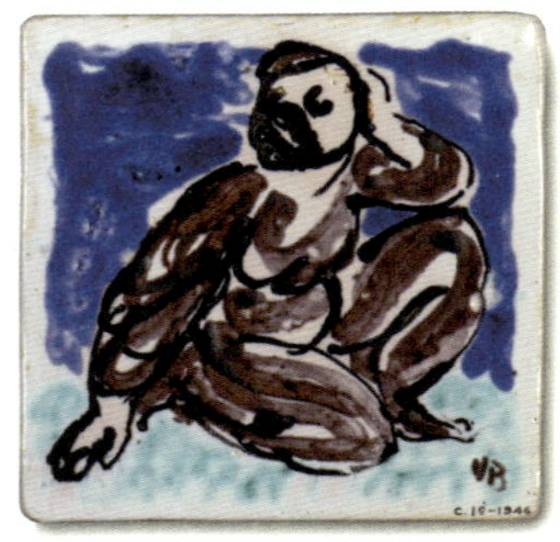

71. Tiles, *c.* 1932
Tin-glazed earthenware,
painted in colours
Victoria and Albert Museum, London
(V&A: C.1&A to C-1946)
Given by Mr Leigh Ashton

Bell painted two portraits of the American actor Miriam Hopkins and one of the Hungarian actor Steffi Duna on these tiles. She may have been reproducing photographs of the stars of stage and screen in relation to the Famous Women dinner service (**fig. 8; 69, 70**). Hopkins had her breakthrough in 1932, the same year that Duna came to London, so both would have received increased publicity. The fourth tile, depicting a kneeling nude figure, bears the mark of potter Phyllis Keyes. It may be unrelated to the portrait tiles, other than the fact that they were all given to the museum by former V&A director Leigh Ashton.

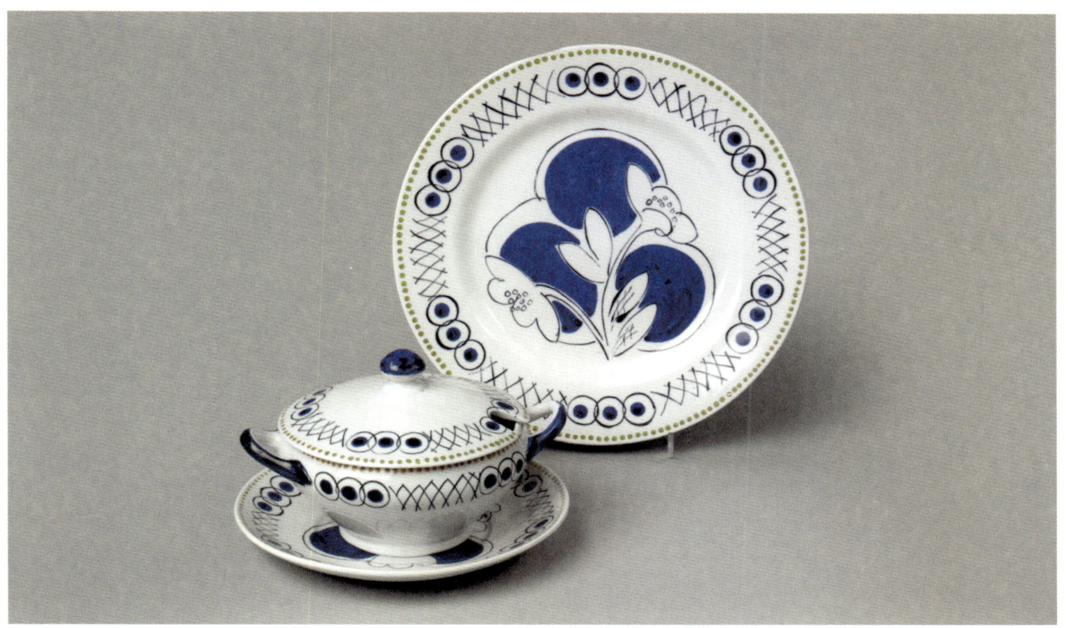

72. Tureen and stand, and plate, 1933–4, made by Arthur J. Wilkinson Ltd, Burslem, Staffordshire
Earthenware, painted in underglaze blue
Victoria and Albert Museum, London (V&A: Misc.2:167 and 168-1934)
Given by Mrs Margaret H. Armitage (née Bulley)

The floral motif and pattern of circles and cross-hatching are typical of Bell but, unlike her unique hand-painted ceramics (**9, 64–67, 70, 71**), this tureen and matching plate in blue and white with delicate green dots were produced as a limited edition by the firm of Arthur J. Wilkinson, following pattern designs by Bell, under Wilkinson's art director Clarice Cliff (1899–1972). They were associated with a project for modern artists to design ceramics and glassware, which were exhibited at Harrods department store in December 1934 in an exhibition entitled *Modern Art for the Table.* Bell participated alongside her daughter Angelica and Grant, as well as twentieth-century British artists including Paul Nash, Barbara Hepworth (1903–1975) and Ben Nicholson (1894–1982).

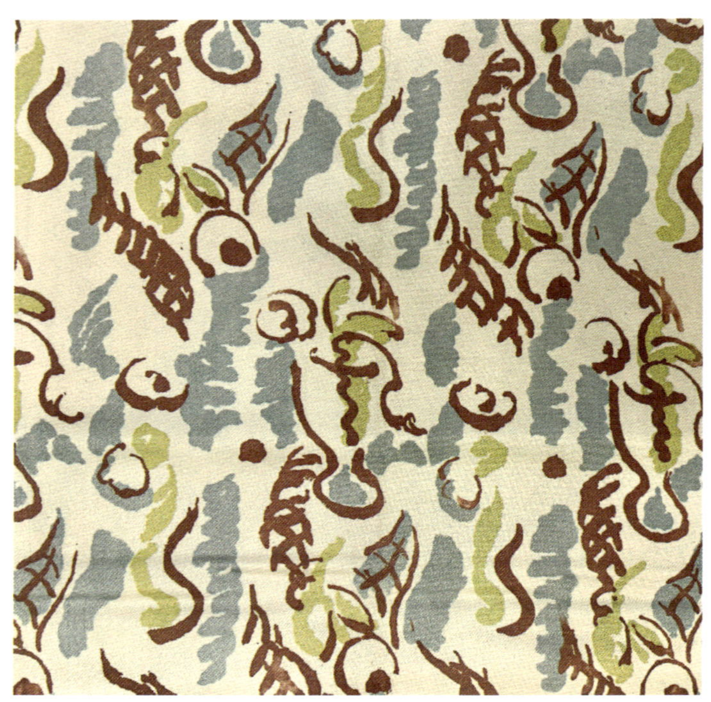

73. Furnishing fabric, 1934, made by Allan Walton Textiles
Printed cotton
Victoria and Albert Museum, London (V&A: Misc.2:176-1934)
Given by Mrs Margaret H. Armitage (née Bulley)

Around 1930 the artist and designer Allan Walton asked Bell, Grant and other modern painters to design textiles. Walton was a fellow member of the London Group, and his family owned a cotton mill in Manchester. When the results were first exhibited at the Cooling Galleries in London, Bell's early design B.18, 'circles and squares in magenta and black, on a grey and white ground', now lost, was highly praised in the *Architectural Review*.[40] Surviving examples such as this, featuring flowers standing in – and possibly tumbling from – a glass, show the more whimsical design typical of Bell (and Grant) in the mid-1930s.

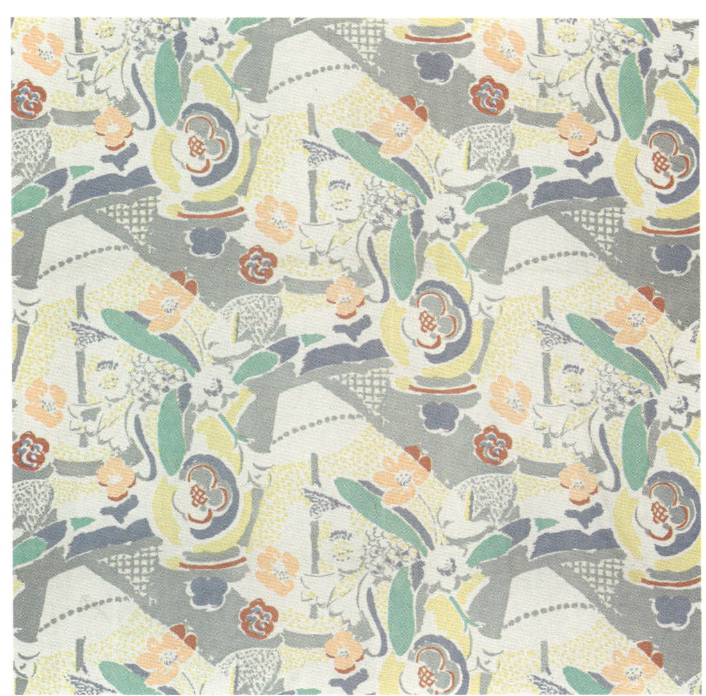

74. Furnishing fabric, 1934,
made by Allan Walton Textiles
Screen-printed satin
Victoria and Albert Museum, London
(V&A: Circ.88A-1937)

This more complex design for Walton shows a floral still life, arranged in a decorated vase similar to those Bell produced with Phyllis Keyes (64, 65). Crucial to the design is a lamp, which casts a yellow light over the vase, represented by Bell with touches of yellow. On the peace lily the same dotted application of colour throws half the bloom into shadow. This alternating yellow and grey, a signature colour scheme, creates a dynamic diagonal force across the pattern.

75. Design for textile, *c.* 1934,
for Allan Walton Textiles
Red ink on paper, 45.2 × 57.2 cm
Victoria and Albert Museum, London
(V&A: E.850-1978)
Given by Mrs D. M. Henderson

This design features an open book, a lamp and a vase of flowers. They are arranged with a spatial complexity typical of Bell's designs for Walton; the lamp seems to sit on a round table, and the flowers appear behind, in the background. Areas of flat colour in comma and T shapes, and cross-hatching, allude to light and shade. However, the unusual use of only one colour gives the design a flatness not characteristic of Bell's textiles for Walton.

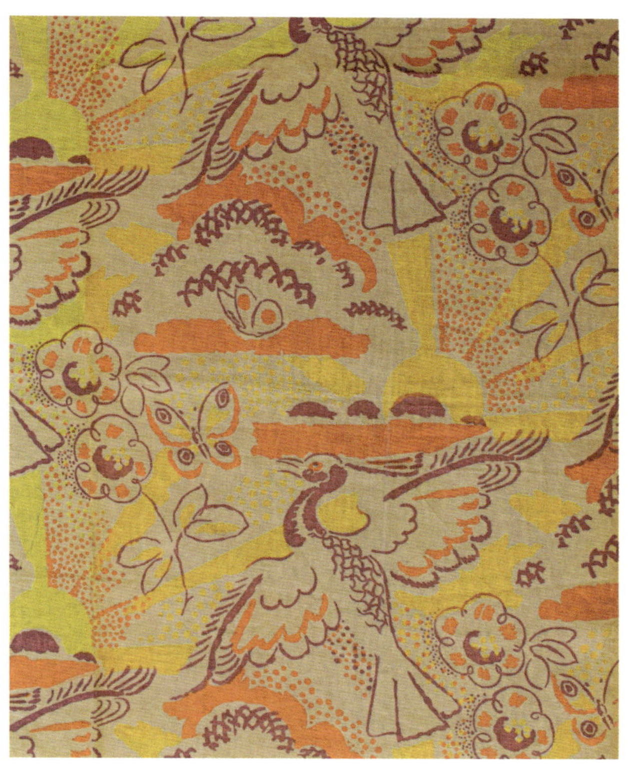

76. 'Birds' furnishing fabric, 1932, made by Allan Walton Textiles
Printed linen
Victoria and Albert Museum, London (V&A: Circ.238-1935)

Bell is better known for depicting flora than fauna, yet this design features large birds and butterflies spreading their wings. It also features a motif similar to Grant's 'Clouds' textile design for Walton in the same year, and Bell's fabric shares Grant's use of freely drawn, looping lines, hatching and stippled colour. The stylized sun in the background of Bell's design is a nod to prevailing art deco tastes. This textile was twice featured in the 1930s London magazine *Decoration.*

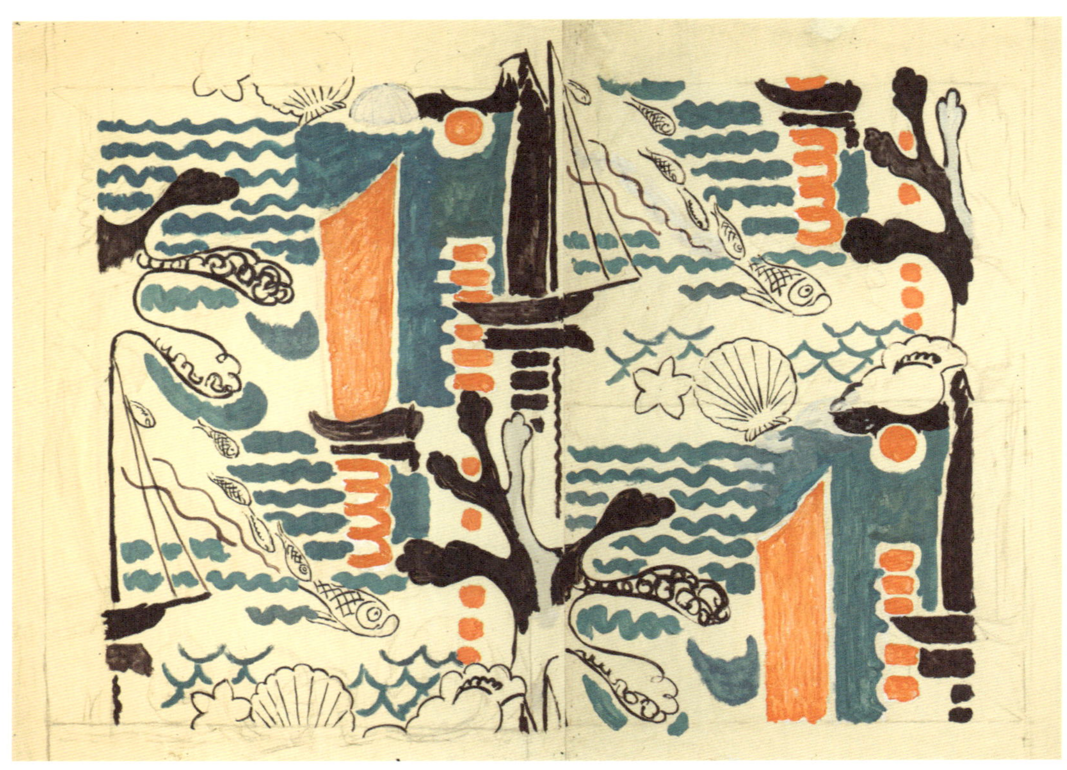

77. Design for textile, *c.* 1934,
for Allan Walton Textiles
Pencil and gouache on paper,
76.2 × 109.2 cm
Victoria and Albert Museum, London
(V&A: E.846 and 847-1978)
Given by Mrs D. M. Henderson

This unusual underwater design reveals how Bell created her complex patterns and distinctive colour schemes. She has joined together two sheets to line up the repeating pattern, with a patch of seaweed overlapping the horizontal axis, and a scallop shell and starfish linking the top and bottom edges. She has freely painted the areas of dark teal that form the waves and the bright coral hue that punctuates it in gouache, an opaque watercolour often used by designers.

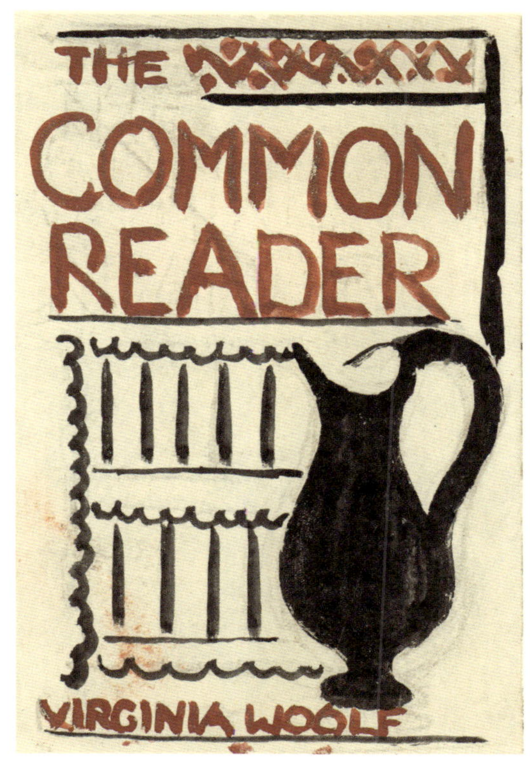

78. Jacket design for *The Common Reader*, by Virginia Woolf, 1925, published by the Hogarth Press
Pencil and gouache on paper, 19.7 × 13.2 cm
Victoria and Albert Museum, London
(V&A: E.223-1981)

Bell's process for designing book jackets was similar to that for creating fabric designs: she would draw in pencil and add colour in gouache, before passing the design to the printer. This initial idea for her sister Virginia Woolf's first book of essays, entitled *The Common Reader*, is close to the final version. The notable exception is the lettering; Bell's own looping handwriting replaced the blocky capital letters she first envisioned. The black gouache on the jug and decorative arrangement in this design would also be changed to a bright green.

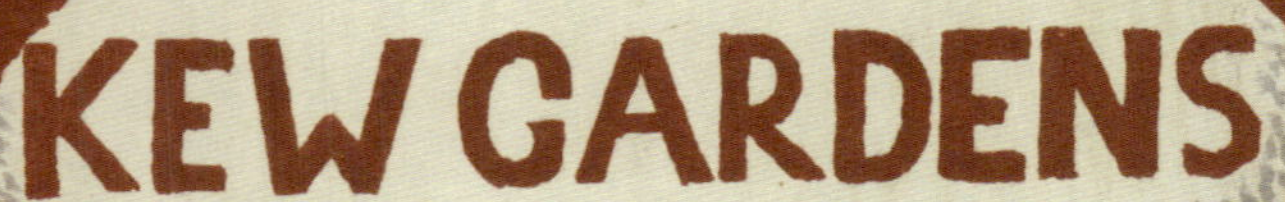
KEW GARDENS
BY
VIRGINIA WOOLF
DECORATIONS
BY
VANESSA BELL
THE
HOGARTH PRESS

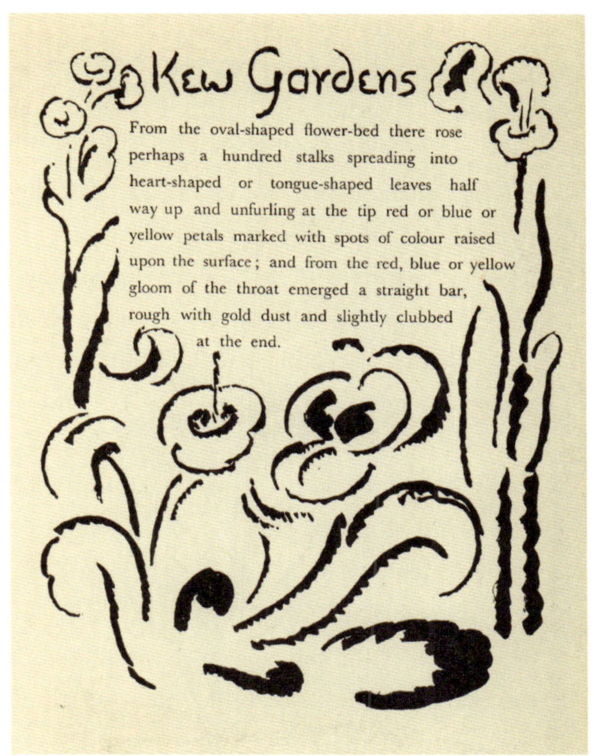
Kew Gardens

From the oval-shaped flower-bed there rose perhaps a hundred stalks spreading into heart-shaped or tongue-shaped leaves half way up and unfurling at the tip red or blue or yellow petals marked with spots of colour raised upon the surface; and from the red, blue or yellow gloom of the throat emerged a straight bar, rough with gold dust and slightly clubbed at the end.

79. Jacket and illustrations for *Kew Gardens*, by Virginia Woolf, 1927, published by the Hogarth Press
Victoria and Albert Museum, London (V&A NAL: 38041981072630)

Bell created a pair of woodcut prints to accompany her sister's short story *Kew Gardens* when it first appeared in the book *Monday or Tuesday* in 1919. When the Hogarth Press published *Kew Gardens* on its own in 1927, she produced an illustration for every page. The highly stylized floral still life on the cover, with foliage spilling over a container, continues to meander across the woodblock prints on subsequent pages, evoking Woolf's own deliberately loose sentences. Among these florals are more ordered designs, recalling the classical temples found at Kew.

The ponderous woman looked through the pattern of falling words at the flowers standing cool, firm and upright in the earth, with a curious expression. She saw them as a sleeper waking from a heavy sleep sees a brass candlestick reflecting the light in an unfamiliar way, and closes his eyes and opens them, and seeing the brass candlestick again, finally starts wide awake and stares at the candlestick with all his powers. So the heavy woman came to a standstill opposite the oval shaped flower bed, and ceased even to pretend to listen to what the other woman was saying. She stood there letting the words fall over her, swaying the top part of her body slowly backwards and forwards, looking at the flowers. Then she suggested that they should find a seat and have their tea.

This time they were both men. The younger of the two wore an expression of perhaps unnatural calm; he raised his eyes and fixed them very steadily in front of him while his companion spoke, and directly his companion had done speaking he looked on the ground again and sometimes opened his lips only after a long pause and sometimes did not open them at all. The elder man had a curiously uneven and shaky method of walking, jerking his hand forward and throwing up his head abruptly, rather in the manner of an impatient carriage horse tired of waiting outside a house; but in the man these gestures were irresolute and pointless. He talked almost incessantly; he smiled to himself, and again began to talk, as if the smile had been an answer.

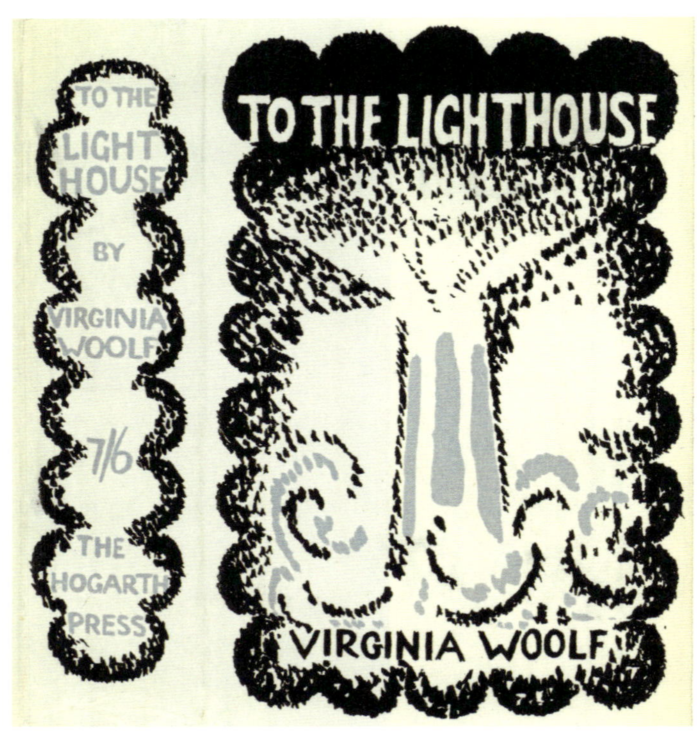

80. Jacket for *To the Lighthouse*, by Virginia Woolf, 1929, published by the Hogarth Press
Archive of Art and Design, Victoria and Albert Museum, London (V&A: AAD/1995/8/03/236)

For this cover Bell embraced the modernist possibilities of the lighthouse as a utilitarian, totemic building, which spans crashing waves to illuminated sky. Bell's use of two shades of blue evokes Woolf's use of the colour within the novel, while her stippled application is indicative of her ongoing use of post-Impressionist techniques to capture the effects of light. The book is partly based on the sisters' childhood holidays staying near a lighthouse at St Ives. It is one of Bell's few unsigned covers for Woolf, prompting the author to write to her, 'I wish you'd signed your cover. Privately I thought it lovely.'[41]

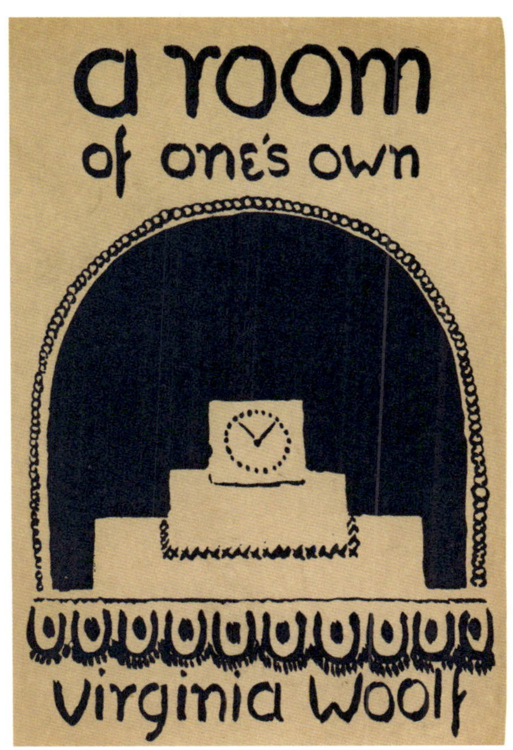

81. Jacket for *A Room of One's Own*, by Virginia Woolf, 1929, published by the Hogarth Press
Victoria and Albert Museum, London
(V&A NAL: 38041988004784)

Bell filled a whole sketchbook with ideas when devising this cover for the published version of Woolf's lectures on women and writing. In the end, she used the image of a geometric, modernist clock, surrounded by a more decorative scheme printed on a peach paper. Woolf wrote to Bell, 'I thought your cover most attractive, but what a stir you'll cause by the hands of the clock at that precise hour!'[42] The V formation, marking the time as 10 minutes to 2, evokes the first names of both artist and author, and Woolf's then lover Vita Sackville-West (1892–1962).

The waves on this cover, behind two silhouetted figures and a floral motif, are ambiguous; they could be literal seascape or decorative wallpaper. The back cover, where a vase of flowers and a book sit on a windowsill, suggests the figures are looking out to sea. Bell did not always read her sister's books before designing the covers. When she submerged herself in this novel, for which she inspired the character of Susan, Bell was very affected by it, writing to Woolf: '[I] am left rather gasping, out of breath choking half drowned as you might expect.'[43]

82. Jacket for *The Waves*, by Virginia Woolf, 1931, published by the Hogarth Press
Archive of Art and Design, Victoria and Albert Museum, London (V&A: AAD/2007/3/0114)

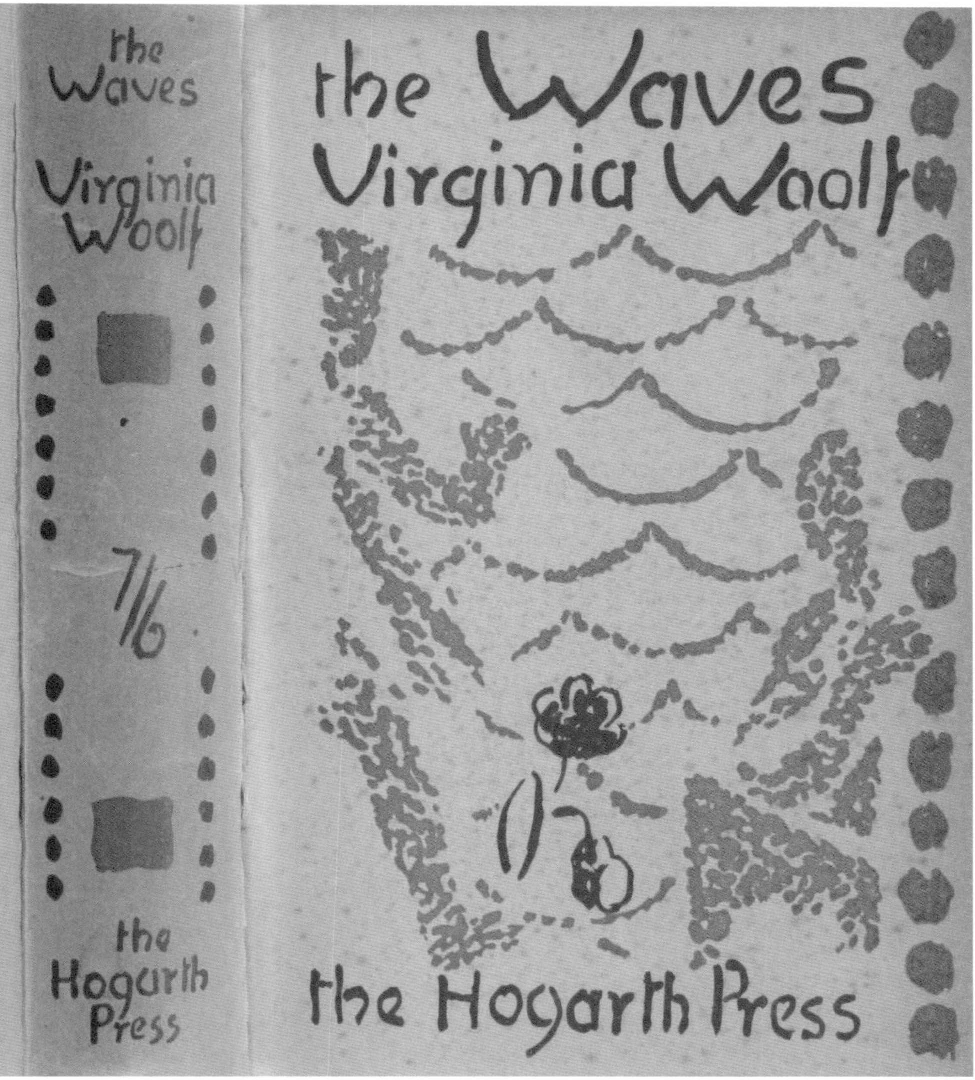

the Waves

Virginia Woolf

7/6

the Hogarth Press

the Waves

Virginia Woolf

the Hogarth Press

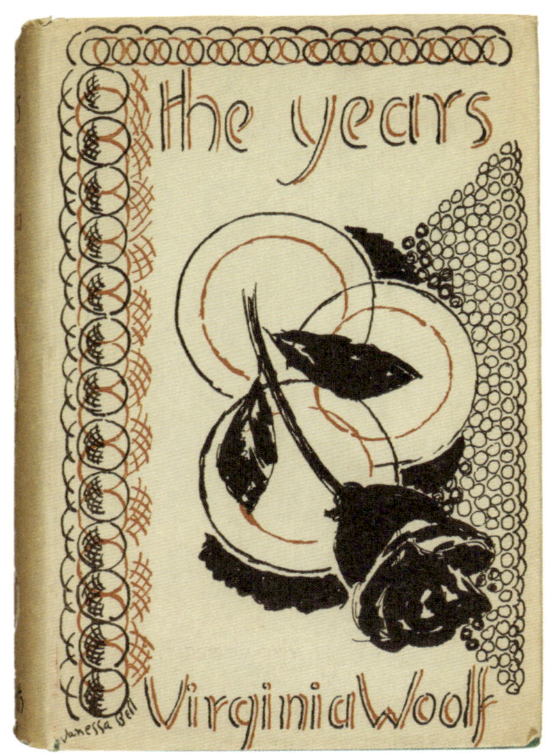

83. Jacket for *The Years*, by Virginia Woolf, 1937, published by the Hogarth Press
Victoria and Albert Museum, London
(V&A NAL: 38041988004800)

This largely abstract design is drawn in black and ruddy brown ink rather than the gouache painting style of earlier designs. It is dominated by the circles and cross-hatching typical of Bell's designs, which also appear on the spine. The rose at the centre of the cover, overlaying three large circles that recall Omega Workshops plates (34), may allude to the name of the youngest daughter of the Pargiter family, whose lives the book chronicles over 50 years. However, floral motifs are common to many of Bell's cover designs, regardless of the story within.

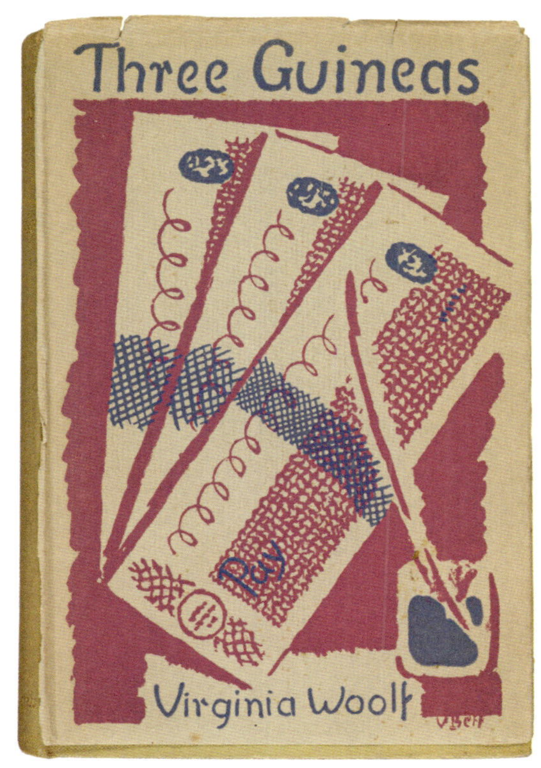

84. Jacket for *Three Guineas*, by Virginia Woolf, 1938, published by the Hogarth Press
Victoria and Albert Museum, London (V&A NAL: L.2901-1988)

The three guineas of this book's title, referring to a trio of occasions on which Woolf was asked for the donation of a guinea, are represented by three blank cheques. These are drawn with Bell's characteristic hatching, circles and looping lines. Bell employed a bold colour palette of magenta and bright blue, and played with perspective, showing the cheques from above and the pen and ink from the side. Unlike *A Room of One's Own* (81), to which this book is a companion piece, Bell has signed her cover at bottom right.

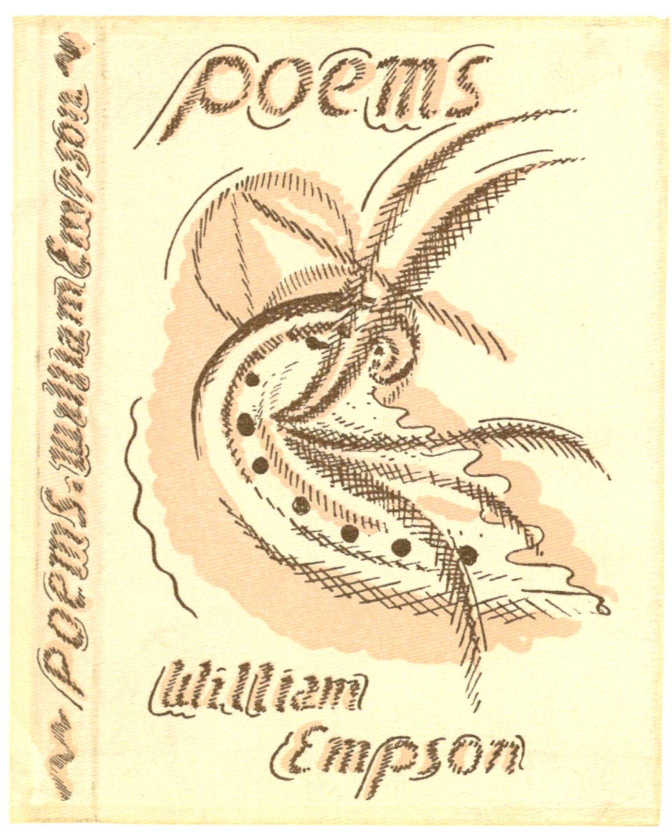

85. Jacket for *Poems*, by William Empson, 1935, published by Chatto & Windus
Victoria and Albert Museum, London
(V&A: E.697-1980)

Bell's finely drawn cover for a book of poetry by William Empson (1906–1984) is dynamic and whimsical. The central motif is a conch shell and the cross-hatched lines used for the text make it seem to quiver. This book was published in the same series as poems by Bell's son, Julian. The Hogarth Press had previously published Empson and Julian Bell together in 1932, and both taught for periods at universities in China.

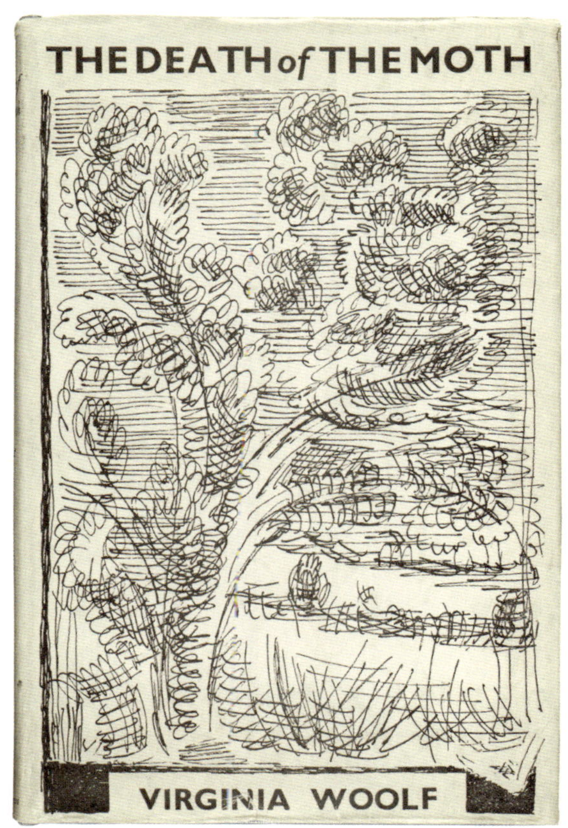

86. Jacket for *The Death of the Moth*, by Virginia Woolf, 1942, published by the Hogarth Press
Victoria and Albert Museum, London (V&A NAL: 38041988004891)

The lyrical pen and ink lines across this cover give a sense of movement to the trees and landscape, which are those around Woolf's Sussex home, Monk's House. The moth itself appears at bottom right, its wings forming a V shape, providing an artist's monogram and alluding to both sisters' names. Bell dedicated much thought to the design of this cover for a book of essays, published posthumously the year after Woolf's death.

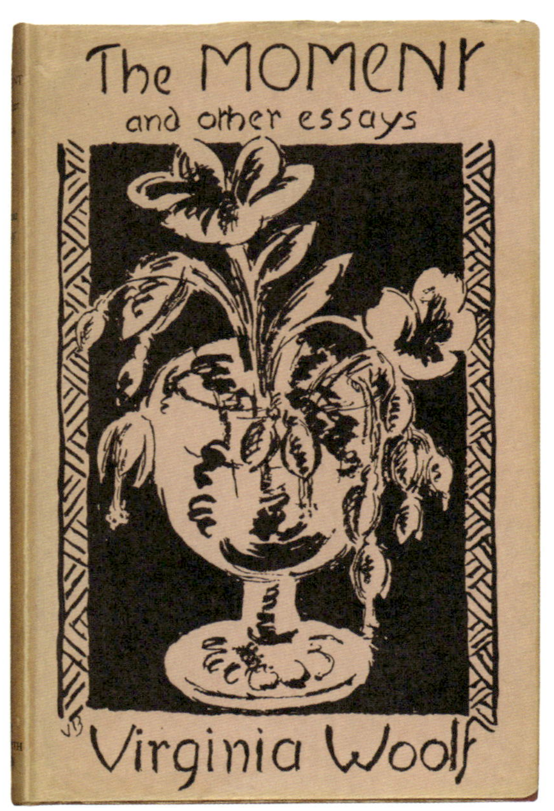

87. Jacket for *The Moment and Other Essays*, by Virginia Woolf, 1942, published by the Hogarth Press
Victoria and Albert Museum, London
(V&A NAL: L.488-1988)

For this posthumous book of Woolf's essays, Bell returned to the motif of the bunch of flowers in a stemmed glass that she had been painting her whole career. Flowers, possibly fuchsias, spill over the side of the glass in a design dominated by black, but printed on pink paper that has since faded. The lettering for the title is distinctive, a carefully constructed mix of straight and curved lines.

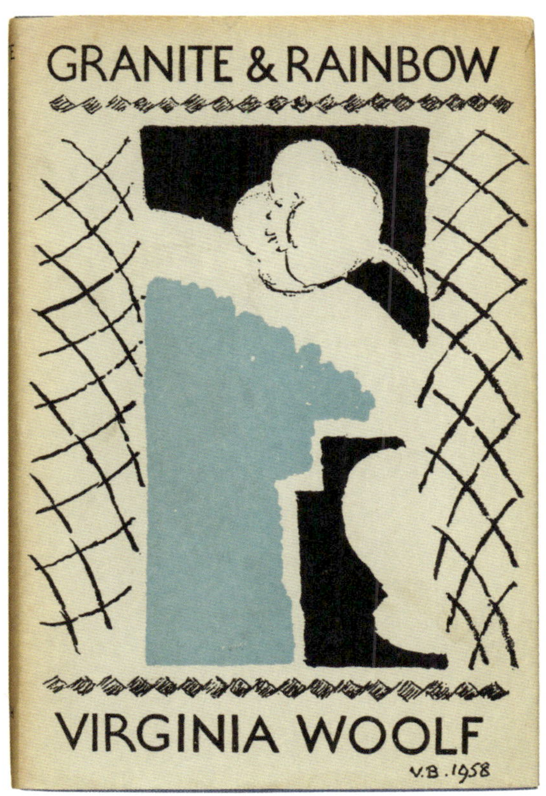

88. Jacket for *Granite & Rainbow*, by Virginia Woolf, 1958, published by the Hogarth Press
Victoria and Albert Museum, London (V&A NAL: 38041800103087)

The last of Bell's book covers shows a remarkable consistency with her work from the 1910s. The central element of the two-colour design, stylized and tightly cropped to the point of abstraction, is a floral arrangement in a room, recalling her *Still Life on Corner of a Mantelpiece* (25) and the associated woodcut *Dahlias* (30). The spine features five cross-hatched ovals, like a set of fingerprints. A notable absence is Bell's own looping lower-case handwriting.

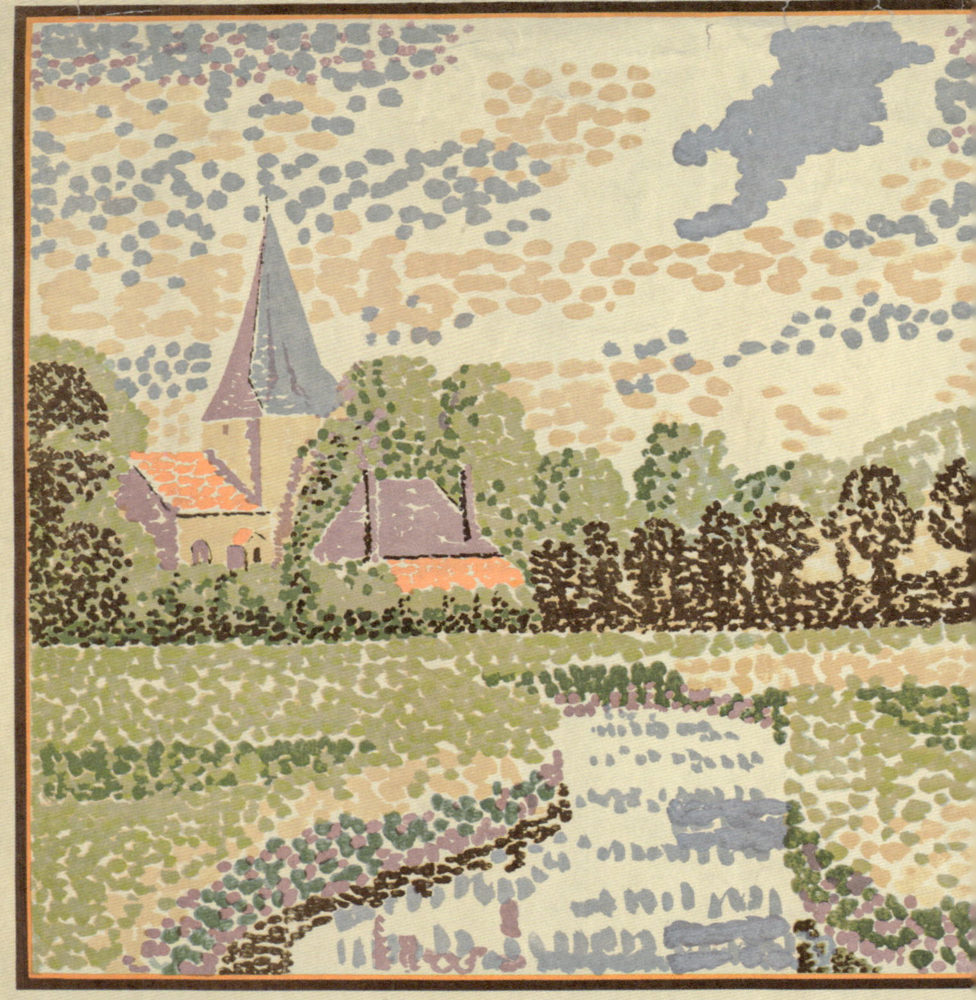
ALFRISTON
SEE BRITAIN FIRST

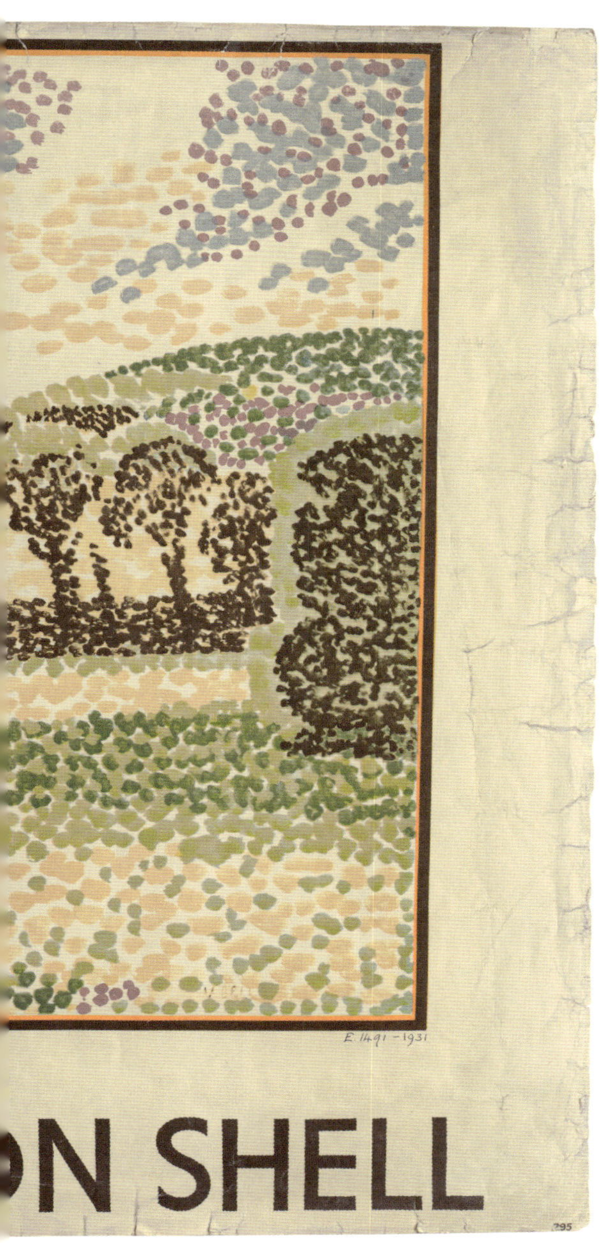

Bell was one of numerous modern artists commissioned by an oil company to produce a series of posters advertising locations that Britain's growing population of motorists might wish to visit. Bell illustrated Alfriston on the South Downs, only a few miles from her home at Charleston, a picturesque village complete with a fourteenth-century church, the winding Cuckmere River and an expansive Sussex sky. Bell built up the images from touches of greens, greys, yellows and browns, with the white of the paper bringing additional brightness.

89. *Alfriston. See Britain First on Shell,* 1931, for Shell-Mex and B.P. Ltd
Colour lithograph, 75.7 × 111.7 cm
Victoria and Albert Museum, London (V&A: E.429-1981)
Given by Roderick Eustace Enthoven

Pattern covers every surface in this image of women writing and playing music in a space of creative domestic calm. It was made to be shown in the home. Commissioned by Contemporary Lithographs, a company founded in 1936 by gallerist Robert Wellington (1910–1990) and artist John Piper (1903–1992), this print was one of fourteen they published in March 1938 aimed 'at making available to households with small incomes a representative and wide choice of good modern work, and is an important step in creating a link between public and art, which is comparable to that between public and literature and music.'[45]

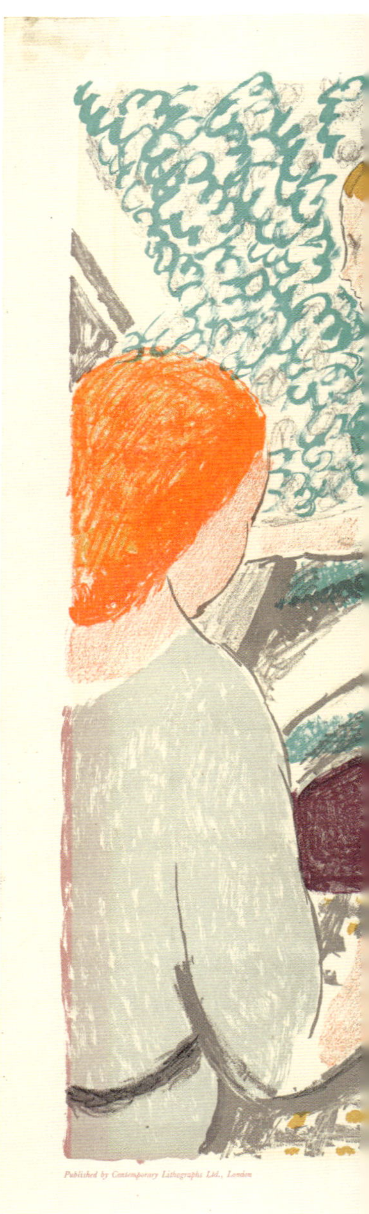

90. *The Schoolroom*, 1938,
for Contemporary Lithographs
Colour lithograph, 50.8 × 66 cm
Victoria and Albert Museum, London
(V&A: Circ.209-1938)

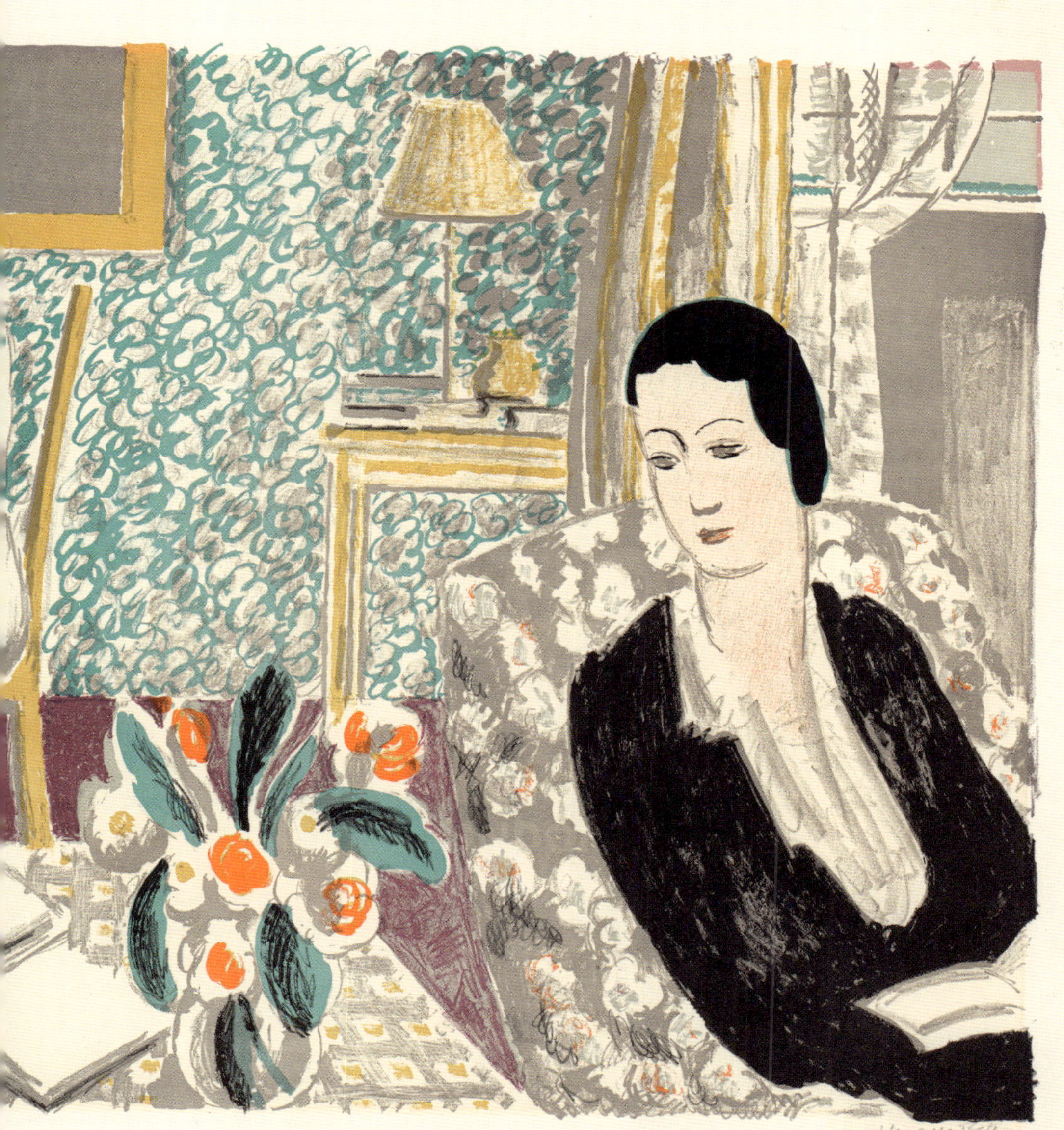

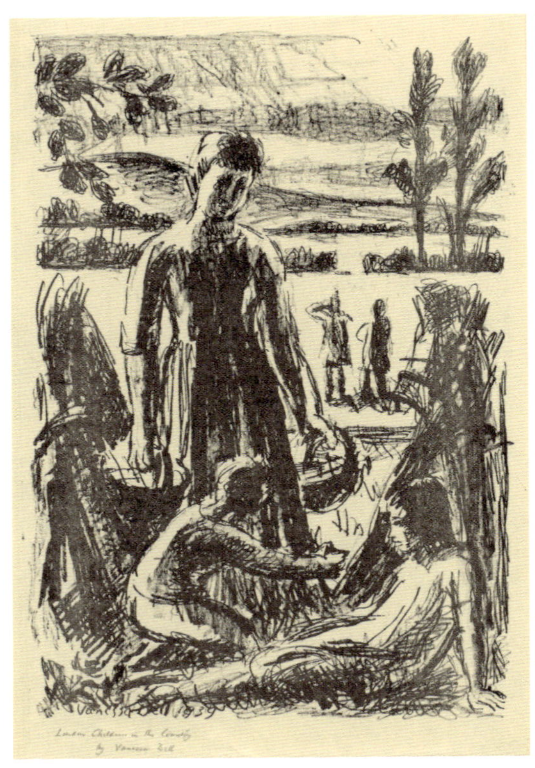

91. *London Children in the Country*, 1939–40, for Artists' International Association
Lithograph, 33.7 × 22.8 cm
Victoria and Albert Museum, London (V&A: E.2214-1948)

This image of children in a Sussex landscape was very likely inspired by Bell's own experiences of raising her family at Charleston during the First World War. Created as the Second World War saw children evacuated from cities, it was published by the Artists' International Association, a group of left-leaning creatives formed in 1933 under the banner 'Unity of Artists for Peace, Democracy and Cultural Development'. This is the fourth print in their Everyman series in which one-colour lithographs like this were sold for one shilling and 'intended for every home'.

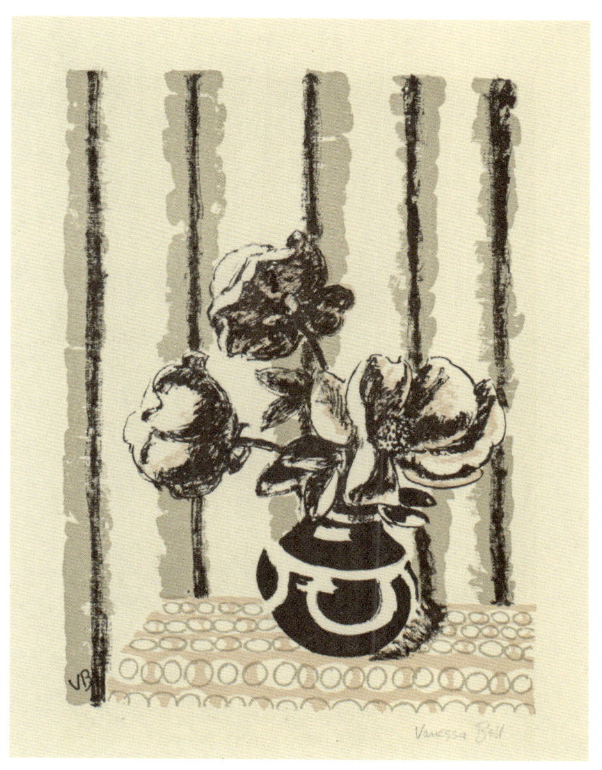

92. *Roses*, 1948
Lithograph, 29.2 × 20.9 cm
Victoria and Albert Museum, London
(V&A: Circ.512-1948)

This print shows Bell at the height of her skill in lithography, capturing texture and pattern in one of her favourite subjects, a floral still life in a domestic interior. The blooms themselves are carefully drawn, with shading to convey their volume, while the vase, rendered in flat geometric colour, is no less convincing in its three-dimensionality. The circles on the tablecloth and stripes on the wall are more freely drawn with varying sizes of lithographic crayon. The palette is remarkably subtle, with dusty pink and a warm grey paired with black.

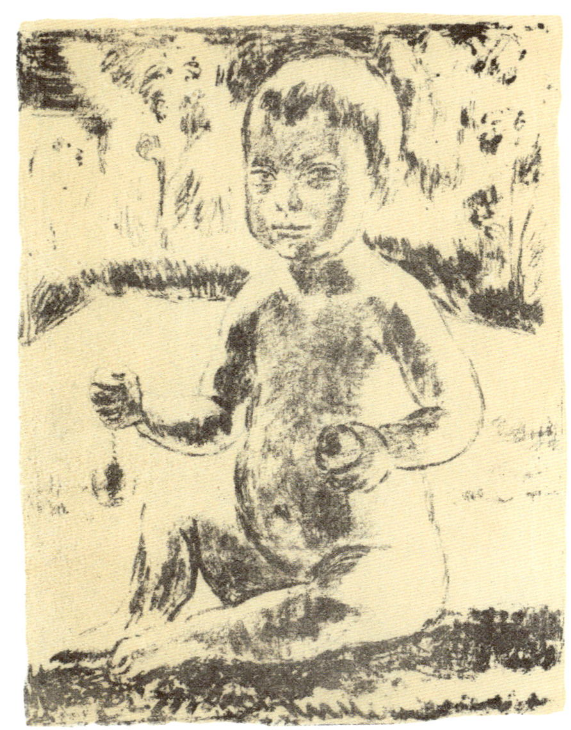

93. *Amaryllis*, 1945
Lithograph, 34.6 × 25.7 cm
Victoria and Albert Museum, London
(V&A: E.92-1945)

94. *Child with a Book*, c. 1946–8
Lithograph, 45 × 35.2 cm
Victoria and Albert Museum, London
(V&A: Circ.511-1948)

Bell's grandchildren were regular models for her, even from a young age. Her first granddaughter appears as a baby in *Amaryllis*, and may reappear in *Child with a Book* a few years later. Both prints are set in the garden at Charleston; the infant is sat naked on the lawn, surrounded by flowerbeds, while the older child, bedecked in a smock and unconvincingly holding a weighty tome, has the farmhouse behind them. The earlier monochrome print is a more immediate snapshot of family life, while the latter is more carefully composed, with a periwinkle blue used to bring depth to the brown-buff ink.

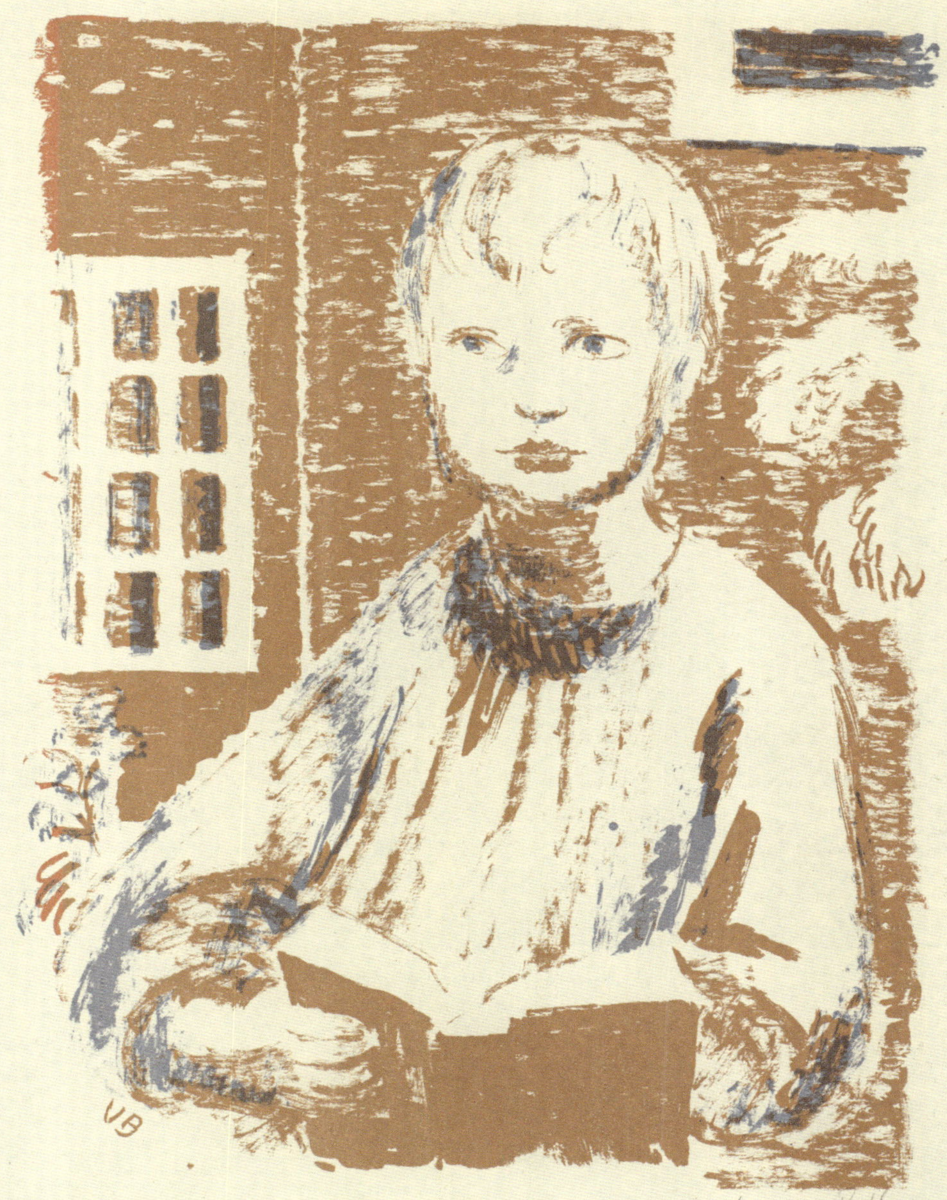
VB
Vanessa Bell

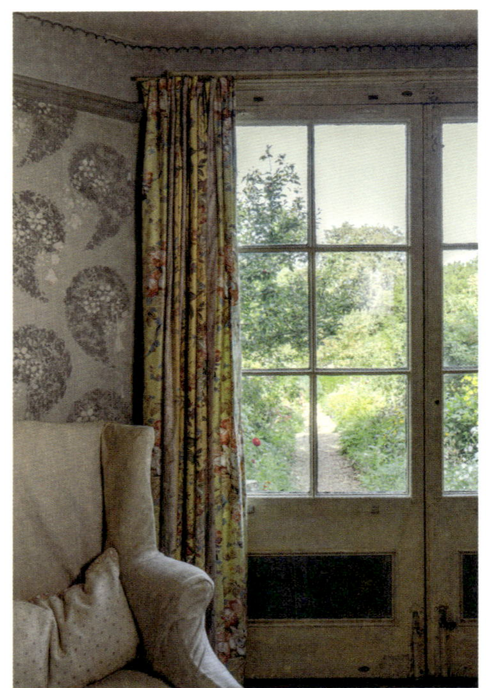

95. The Garden Room at Charleston

96. *Girl Reading*, 1945, for Miller's Press
Lithograph, 33 × 25.4 cm
Victoria and Albert Museum, London
(V&A: E.93-1945)

A young woman absorbed in a book adopts a pose much like Bell's painting of her daughter Angelica from the previous decade (45). The figure has been transposed from the Studio to the Garden Room at Charleston. Although starkly geometric, elements of the room are recognizable: the grid of the French doors, the shape of a screen by Grant, and the grey walls, painted by Bell and Grant that October with dark grey comma shapes (95). The print was commissioned by sisters Frances Byng-Stamper (1882–1968) and Caroline Lucas (1886–1967) who set up the Miller's Press in Lewes in 1945 to revitalize the art of lithography.

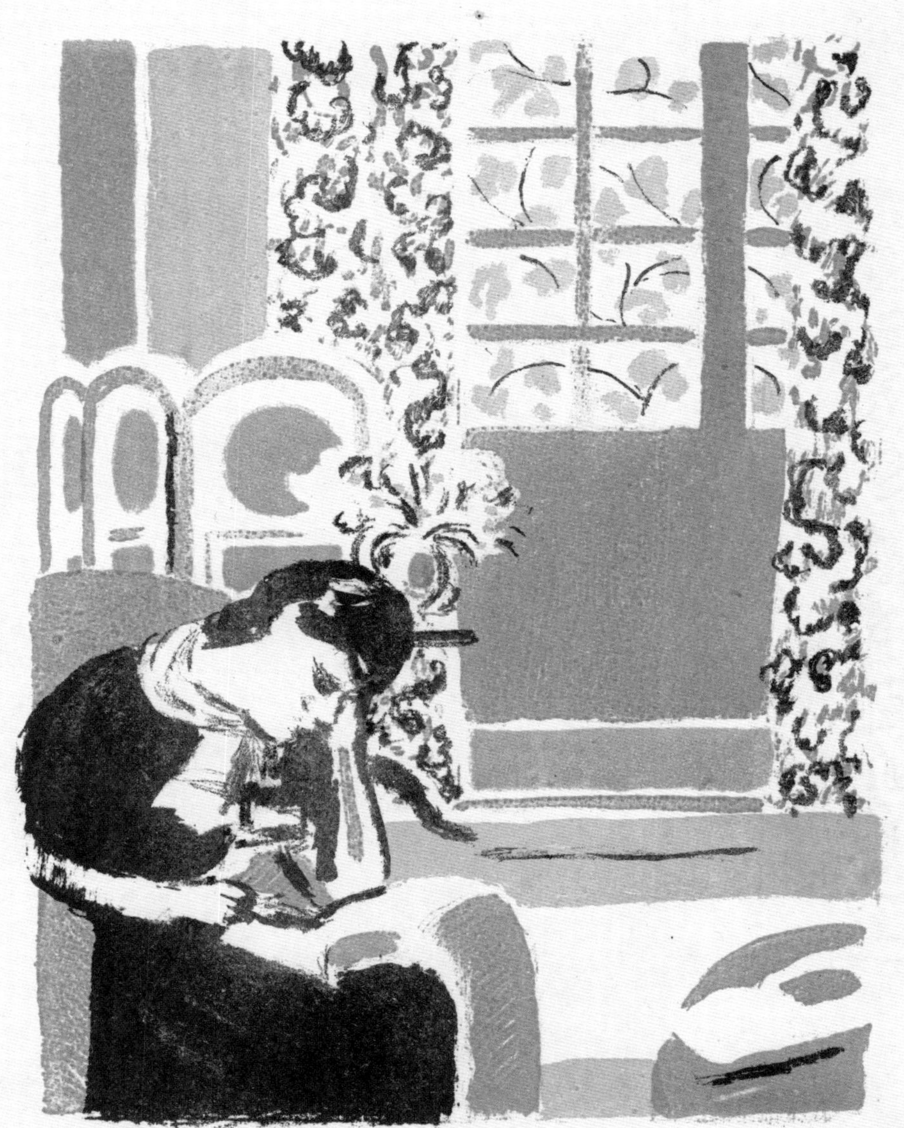
VB

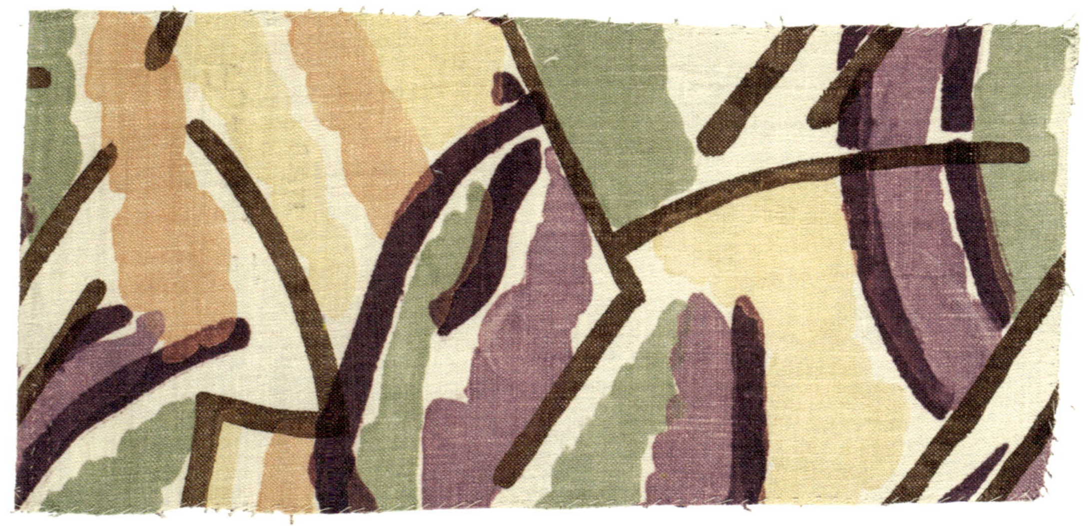

97. Duncan Grant, 'Pamela' textile, 1913, made by Besselièvre for Omega Workshops Ltd
Printed linen
Victoria and Albert Museum, London (V&A: Circ.6-1932)
Given by Miss M. Hogarth

98. *Woman with a Book*, 1948, for Miller's Press
Lithograph, 50.8 × 35.5 cm
Victoria and Albert Museum, London (V&A: Circ.105-1950)

This print of a woman, with downcast eyes and a book on her lap, was based on a painting by Bell. In the print, the painting's decorative elements – the delicate flowers on her scarf and the bold foliage of the background – have been simplified. In the painting, the backdrop resembles Grant's 'Queen M' textile for Allan Walton, while in the print it is closer to his 'Pamela' textile for the Omega Workshops in its purple, green and ochre colourway (97). In 1946 Miller's Press held an exhibition of Omega products at their gallery in Lewes.

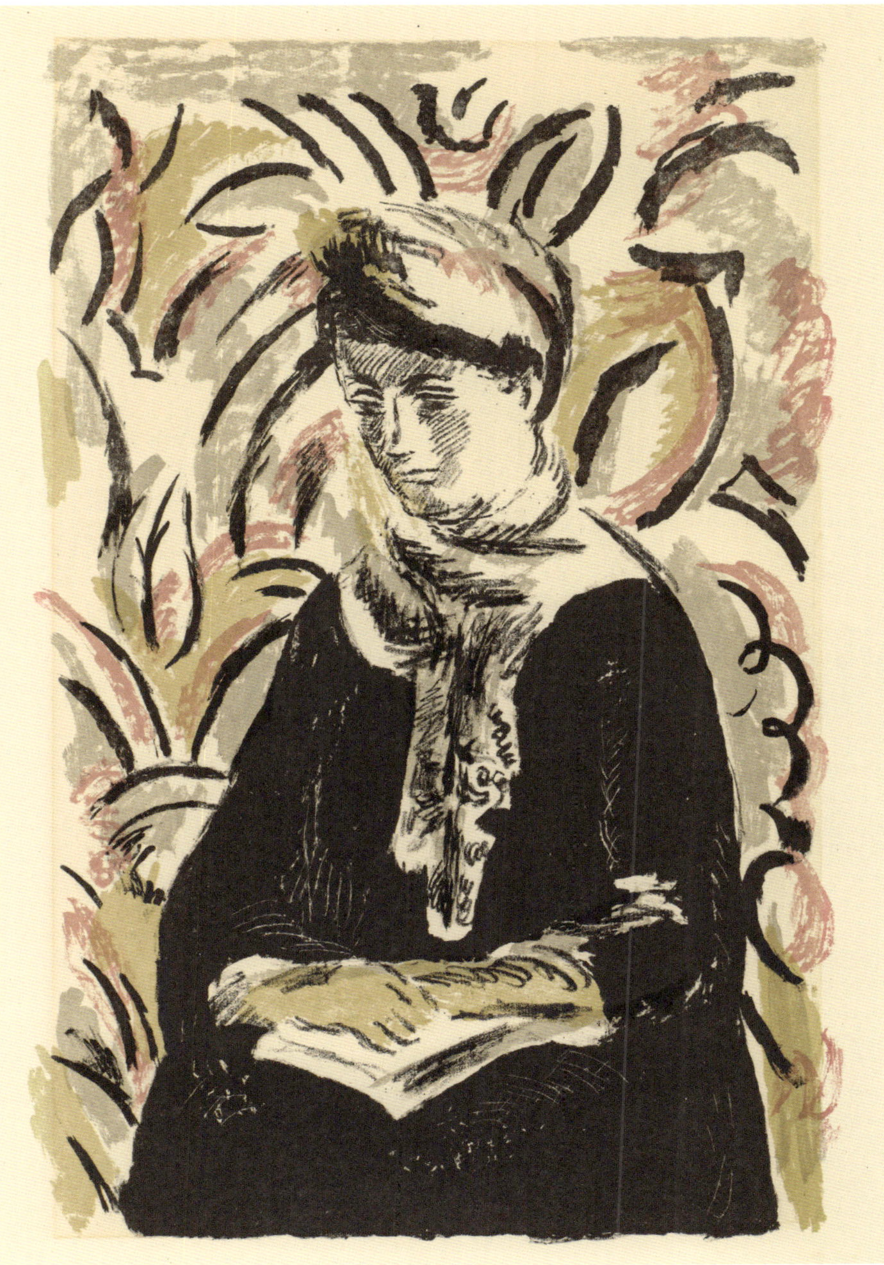

Notes

1 Vanessa Bell to Virginia Stephen, 31 July 1907, quoted in Marler 1993, p. 52.
2 R.R. Tatlock, 'The London Group', *Burlington Magazine for Connoisseurs*, 43:248 (November 1923), p. 250.
3 Virginia Woolf, 'Foreword', *Recent Paintings by Vanessa Bell* (London, 1930), n.p.
4 Vanessa Bell to Angelica Bell, 24 November 1941, quoted in Spalding 1983, p. 320.
5 On Bell's critical fortunes see Brockington 2013.
6 Bell remembered 'darkness and silence' as the house's chief characteristics. Vanessa Bell, 'Life at Hyde Park Gate after 1897', in Giachero 1997, p. 81.
7 Vanessa Bell, 'Notes on Virginia's Childhood', in Giachero 1997, p. 63.
8 Bell, 'Life at Hyde Park Gate after 1897', p. 75.
9 Ibid., pp. 73–4.
10 Mauclair 1903.
11 Vanessa Bell, 'Notes on Bloomsbury', in Giachero 1997, pp. 98–9.
12 Woolf, *Diaries*, vol. III, p. 124; quoted in Spalding 1983, p. 215.
13 Vanessa Bell, 'Memories of Roger Fry', in Giachero 1997, p. 130.
14 Virginia Woolf, 'Mr. Bennett and Mrs. Brown', *Collected Essays* (New York, 1967), vol. I, pp. 320–1.
15 *Asheham* and *The Mantelpiece* were probably interiors; the other women artists were Jessie Etchells, Rena Hassenberg (1884–1953), Sophie Lewitzka (1880–1937) and Jacqueline-Marie Marval (1866–1932).
16 Spalding 1983, p. 113.
17 'Professor Quentin Bell in Conversation with Duncan Grant', in Simon Watney, *The Art of Duncan Grant* (London, 1990), pp. 81–7, at p. 85.
18 Vanessa Bell to Roger Fry, 27 April 1916, quoted in Dunn 2000, p. 219.
19 Clive Bell to Vanessa Bell, Monday [24 June 1918?], in Hussey 2023, pp. 207–8.
20 Vanessa Bell to Duncan Grant, September 1916, Tate Archive, quoted in Spalding 1997, pp. 190–1.
21 Vanessa Bell to Duncan Grant, 3 August 1921, King's College Cambridge, quoted in Spalding 1983, p. 190.
22 McNeill 1994.
23 Tate Archive, TGA 20078/8/1/4.
24 'Modern English Decoration: Some Examples of the Interesting Work of Duncan Grant and Vanessa Bell', *Vogue* (Early November 1924), p. 45.
25 Hermione Lee, *Virginia Woolf* (London, 1997), p. 367. See also Jenni Råback's paper, 'Covering for Her Sister: Vanessa Bell's "Completely Upsetting" Dust-Jackets', given at the symposium 'Decorating Dissidence: Modernism, Feminism and the Arts' at Queen Mary, University of London, November 2017.
26 Vanessa Bell to Roger Fry, 18 September 1913, Tate Archive, quoted in Marler 1993, p. 144.
27 Fry 1915, p. 10.
28 Winifred Gill to Duncan Grant, June 1966, Tate Archive, quoted in Gerstein 2009, p. 147.
29 Virginia Woolf to Vanessa Bell, August 1916, quoted in Woolf, *Letters*, vol. II, p. 111.
30 Vanessa Bell to Duncan Grant, 29 January 1914, Tate Archive.
31 Vanessa Bell to Roger Fry, 2 April 1913, quoted in Gerstein 2009, p. 112.
32 Bell 1914, p. 23.
33 Vanessa Bell, 'Lecture Given at Leighton Park School', in Giachero 1997, pp. 161–2.
34 Greenwood 1998, p. 22.
35 Vanessa Bell to Winifred Gill, 2 November 1918 [?], National Art Library, Victoria and Albert Museum, London (MSL/1967/5226).
36 Vanessa Bell to Duncan Grant, 18 September 1916, British Library, quoted in Spalding 1983, p. 155.

37 'Modern English Decoration: Some Examples of the Interesting Work of Duncan Grant and Vanessa Bell', *Vogue* (Early November 1924), p. 43.
38 'The Work of Modern Decorative Artists', *Vogue* (Late August 1926), p. 29.
39 Vanessa Bell to Roger Fry, October 1931 quoted in Spalding 1983, p. 242; Clark 1974, p. 248.
40 Cyril Connolly, 'Genuine Arts and Crafts', *Architectural Review* (January 1932), p. 23.
41 Virginia Woolf to Vanessa Bell, 8 June [?] 1927, quoted in Spalding 1983, p. 222; Woolf, *Letters*, vol. III, p. 391.
42 Woolf, *Letters*, vol. IV, p. 81.
43 Vanessa Bell to Virginia Woolf, October 1931, Berg Collection, New York Public Library, quoted in Spalding 1983, p. 251.
44 Virginia Woolf to Vanessa Bell, 8 June [?] 1927, quoted in Spalding 1983, p. 222; Woolf, *Letters*, vol. III, p. 391.
45 'Contemporary Lithographs', *The Studio* (December 1938), p. 301.

Picture Credits

Unless otherwise noted, all works reproduced are in the V&A collection and photographed by the V&A Photo Studio / Ed Lyon / Kieron Boyle.

All Vanessa Bell works are © Estate of Vanessa Bell / All rights reserved, DACS 2024. All Duncan Grant works are © Estate of Duncan Grant / All rights reserved, DACS 2024.

Fig. 10 and pls 2, 3,15,19, 28, 35, 38, 45, 49, 54, 56, 64 were provided by The Charleston Trust; fig. 8 and pls 69, 70 courtesy The Charleston Trust © Piano Nobile. Photography of Charleston and its garden (pls 1, 41, 42, 43, 44, 46, 48, 50, 51, 95) by Peter Kelleher for the V&A with kind permission of The Charleston Trust.

Additional copyright holders and image lenders: Image courtesy Yale Center for British Art fig. 1; Image © GrandPalaisRmn (musée d'Orsay) / Hervé Lewandowski fig. 4; © Tate; photo: Tate fig. 7; © IMEC, Fonds MCC, Dist. GrandPalaisRmn / Gisèle Freund fig. 9; Image © Art Gallery of South Australia, Adelaide pl. 5; Image courtesy Yale Center for British Art pl. 6; Image © National Portrait Gallery, London pl. 7; © TfL from the London Transport Museum collection pl. 11; Image courtesy Yale Center for British Art pl. 14; Photo: Todd-White Art Photography, London pl. 23; Image courtesy University of Leeds Art Collection (LEEUA1923.1) pl. 24; Photo: Tate pl. 25; Photo: Tate pl. 26; Courtesy SMK, National Gallery of Denmark / Photo: © SMK/Jacob Schou-Hansen pl. 32; Photo: Tate pl. 33; Image courtesy of Museum & Art Swindon pl. 36; Image courtesy Williamson Art Gallery & Museum pl. 47; By permission of the Provost and Scholars of King's College, Cambridge pl. 52; © Architectural Press Archive / RIBA Collections RIBA Ref No: RIBA52388; Charleston Trust pl. 53

Selected Bibliography

This bibliography lists works referenced in the notes as well as titles for wider reading.

Isabelle Anscombe, *Omega and After: Bloomsbury and the Decorative Arts* (London, 1981)

Clive Bell, *Art* (London, 1914)

Quentin Bell, *Charleston: A Bloomsbury House and Garden* (London, 1997)

Grace Brockington, 'A "Lavender Talent" or "The Most Important Woman Painter in Europe"? Reassessing Vanessa Bell', *Art History*, 36:1 (February 2013), pp. 128–53

Kenneth Clark, *Another Part of the Wood: A Self-Portrait* (London, 1974)

Darren Clarke (ed.), *Post-Impressionist Living: The Omega Workshops* (Firle, East Sussex, 2019)

David Cottington, *Radical Art and the Formation of the Avant-Garde* (London and New Haven, 2022)

Jane Dunn, *Virginia Woolf and Vanessa Bell: A Very Close Conspiracy* (London, 2000)

Roger Fry, *Omega Workshops Descriptive Catalogue* (London, 1915)

Alexandra Gerstein (ed.), *Beyond Bloomsbury: Designs of the Omega Workshops 1913–19* (London, 2009)

Lia Giachero (ed.), *Sketches in Pen and Ink: A Bloomsbury Notebook* (London, 1997)

Jeremy Greenwood, *Omega Cuts* (Woodbridge, Suffolk, 1998)

Wendy Hitchmough, *The Bloomsbury Look* (New Haven, 2020)

Mark Hussey, *Selected Letters of Clive Bell: Art, Love and War in Bloomsbury* (Edinburgh, 2023)

Regina Marler (ed.), *Selected Letters of Vanessa Bell* (London, 1993)

Camille Mauclair, *The French Impressionists*, trans. P.G. Konody (London, 1903)

Peter McNeill, 'Designing Women: Gender, Sexuality and the Interior Decorator, c.1890–1940', *Art History*, 17:4 (December 1994), pp. 631–57

Sarah Milroy and Ian Dejardin, *Vanessa Bell* (London, 2017)

Nigel Nicholson (ed.), *A Change of Perspective: The Letters of Virginia Woolf, Vol. III: 1923–1928* (London, 1977)

Nigel Nicholson (ed.), *A Reflection of the Other Person: The Letters of Virginia Woolf, Vol. IV: 1929–1931* (London, 1978)

Derek Patmore, *Colour Schemes for the Modern Home* (London and New York, 1933)

Christopher Reed, *Bloomsbury Rooms: Modernism, Subculture, and Domesticity* (New Haven, 2004)

Richard Shone, *The Art of Bloomsbury* (London, 1999)

Richard Shone, 'The Friday Club', *Burlington Magazine*, 117:866 (May 1975), pp. 274–84

Richard Shone, *From Omega to Charleston: The Art of Vanessa Bell and Duncan Grant 1910–1934* (London, 2018)

Frances Spalding, *Vanessa Bell: Portrait of the Bloomsbury Artist* (London, 1983)

Frances Spalding, *Duncan Grant* (London, 1997)

Pamela Todd, *Bloomsbury at Home* (London, 1999)

Dorothy Todd and Raymond Mortimer, *The New Interior Decoration: An Introduction to its Principles, and International Survey of its Methods* (London, 1929)

Acknowledgments

I wish to thank all those whose writings and conversations have shaped this book. Among those listed in the bibliography, the work of Christopher Reed and Frances Spalding has been critical to its development, and Wendy Hitchmough was an insightful and generous reader. This book is dedicated to the memory of David Cottington, with whom I would have loved to talk about it.

My work on this book has been greatly enriched by Nathaniel Hepburn, Darren Clarke and Miriam Phelan at Charleston, by Max Donnelly, Alun Graves and Jessica Harpley at the V&A, and by Hannah Newell and Becca Fortey in V&A Publishing. Lastly, my thanks to James Leigh and Kate Piper for their hospitality during my research trips, and to everyone, especially Anthony Leigh, who endured my talking of nothing but Vanessa.

Author's Biography

Dr Rosalind McKever is Curator of Paintings and Drawings at the V&A and specializes in modern European art, its reception in Britain and North and South America, and its relationship with fashion and design. She has previously worked at the National Gallery, London, and the Metropolitan Museum of Art, New York. She studied History of Art with Italian at the University of Leeds, obtained her PhD on Italian Futurism's relationship with the past at Kingston University in collaboration with the Estorick Collection of Modern Italian Art, and has taught art history at the University of Sussex.

Front cover image: Detail from *The Schoolroom*, 1938 (pp. 130–1)
Back cover image: Detail from 'Maud' textile, 1913 (p. 50)
Opposite title page: Detail of *Interior with the Artist's Daughter*, *c.* 1935–6 (p. 80)
Opposite contents page: Detail of design for a textile, 1913 (p. 45)

First published in the United Kingdom in 2025 by
Thames & Hudson Ltd, 181A High Holborn, London WC1V 7QX
in association with the Victoria and Albert Museum, London

First published in the United States of America in 2025 by
Thames & Hudson Inc., 500 Fifth Avenue, New York, New York 10110

British Library Cataloguing-in-Publication Data
A catalogue record for this book is available from the British Library

Library of Congress Control Number 2024946206

ISBN 978-0-500-48105-9

Impression 01

Printed and bound in China by C&C Offset Printing Co. Ltd

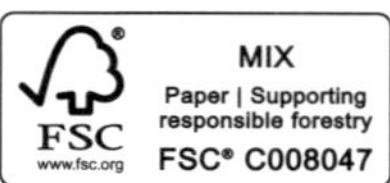

V&A Publishing

Supporting the world's leading
museum of art and design,
the Victoria and Albert
Museum, London